OTHER BOOKS BY ROLAND BARTHES

A Barthes Reader
Camera Lucida
Critical Essays
The Eiffel Tower and Other Mythologies
Elements of Semiology
The Empire of Signs
The Fashion System
The Grain of the Voice
Image-Music-Text
A Lover's Discourse
Mythologies
New Critical Essays
On Racine
The Pleasure of the Text
The Responsibility of Forms
Roland Barthes
The Rustle of Language
Sade / Fourier / Loyola
S / Z
Writing Degree Zero

MICHELET

Michelet

ROLAND BARTHES

TRANSLATED BY
R I C H A R D   H O W A R D

UNIVERSITY OF CALIFORNIA PRESS
Berkeley • Los Angeles

University of California Press
Berkeley and Los Angeles, California
First California Paperback Printing 1992

Translation copyright © 1987 by Farrar, Straus and Giroux, Inc.
Originally published in French, copyright © 1954 by Editions du Seuil
ALL RIGHTS RESERVED
Printed in the United States of America
Designed by Tina Kachele

Jacket illustration of Michelet by Couture: Giraudon/Art Resource, NY

Interior illustrations: pp. viii, 31, 89, 111, 180, 181, Roger-Viollet;
p. 2, Archives Photographiques; pp. 11 (top), 26, 108, 130, 176, 204, 205,
Bulloz; p. 40, Rigal; p. 6, Musée Carnavalet;
by arrangement with Editions du Seuil

Library of Congress Cataloging-in-Publication Data
Michelet, Jules, 1798–1874.
[Michelet par lui-même. English]
Michelet / [edited by] Roland Barthes;
translated by Richard Howard.
p. cm.
Originally published: New York: Hill and Wang, 1987.
Translation of: Michelet par lui-même.
ISBN 0-520-07826-8
1. Michelet, Jules, 1798–1874.   2. Historians—France—Biography.
3. France—Historiography.   I. Barthes, Roland.   II. Title.
[DC36.98.M5A3   1992]
944'.007202—dc20
[B]
91-39229
CIP

9   8   7   6   5   4   3   2   1

CONTENTS

15 D. 57 '59

Cher monsieur

Depuis que je suis revenu, j'ai
voulu chaque dimanche aller vous
voir, et je n'ai le puis. je suis à Véni
et tout près, ne quittant pas ma
femme qui a été *très malade* —

Je serai bien reconnaissant si
vous voulez bien me dire comment
va madame — je vous appartiens
à tous deux, noyez le, et de cœur —
Ma femme vous salue affectueusement
                                    J. Michelet

I am a complete man, having
both sexes of the mind.
                                    —Michelet

MICHELET

Michelet
Photograph by Nadar

In this little book, the reader will find neither a history of Michelet's thought nor a history of his life—still less an explanation of the former by the latter.

That Michelet's oeuvre, like any object of criticism, is ultimately the product of a certain history, I am quite convinced. But there is an order of tasks: first of all, we must restore to this man his coherence. That has been my endeavor: to recover the structure of an existence (if not of a life), a thematics, if you like, or better still: an organized network of obsessions. Then will come the real critics, historians or phenomenologists or psychoanalysts: the present work is no more than pre-criticism. I have sought merely to describe a unity, not to explore its roots in history or in biography.

As for the illustrations, I have chosen them with respect to the man, rather than to his life or his times: I have included virtually all the images of Michelet there are, and beyond that—inspired by the impassioned gaze he fastened upon any and every historical object—I have freely chosen several exhibits from what might be called Michelet's *Musée imaginaire*.

The Dumesnil house at Vascoeil, on the banks
of the Andelle, where Michelet often stayed

MEMORANDUM

MICHELET (Jules), French historian, born in Paris. His liberal opinions twice caused his lectures at the Collège de France to be suspended. In his *Histoire de France* and his *Histoire de la Révolution,* he managed to effect a veritable resurrection of our national life (1798–1874).   —Petit Larousse illustré, 1906–34

CHRONOLOGY

"I was born during the great territorial revolution, and I shall have seen the dawn of the great industrial revolution. Born under the Terror of Babeuf, I see, before I die, the Terror of the Internationale."

ANCESTRY

The Michelets of Laon. A family of artisans.

His father, Furcy Michelet: a journeyman printer; later, ruined by Napoleon, manager of an asylum; a Voltairean and a supporter of the Republic, he served as a guard at the Temple.

The Millets of Renwez (Ardennes). A very pious mother.

EDUCATION

Secondary studies at the Lycée Charlemagne
1816   Three prizes in the *Concours général*

1817   Bachelier
1818   Licencié
1819   Docteur ès Lettres
1821   Third place in the *Agrégation des Lettres* (state competition)

CAREER

1821   Assigned to Lycée Charlemagne as *agrégé volant* (supplementary staff)
1822   Assistant lecturer in history at the new Collège Sainte-Barbe, later the Collège Rollin
1827   Lecturer at the École Normale Supérieure (then known as the École Préparatoire)
1828   Tutor to the daughter of the Duchesse de Berry
1830   Tutor to the Princesse Clémentine, daughter of Louis-Philippe. Head of the Historical Section of the National Archives
1831   Chief lecturer at the Faculté des Lettres
1834   Replaces Guizot at the Sorbonne
1838   Professor at the Collège de France, Chair of History and Ethics. Member of the Institut

[6]

1843 Resigns as tutor to the princess
1851 Michelet's lectures suspended at the Collège de France
1852 Refuses allegiance to Napoleon III. Dismissal as archivist
From 1852 until his death, Michelet lives in considerable poverty,
      first near Nantes, then in Paris (rue d'Assas). During this
      last part of his life, Michelet and his wife make many jour-
      neys in France, Switzerland, and Italy.

INFLUENCES

Vico, the Scottish philosophers, the German historians (Momm-
sen, Ganz, Niebuhr, Jacob Grimm), the French eighteenth century.

LOVES

Three women in Michelet's life, not counting a mistress (Madame Aubépin) and some ancillary loves, Rustica and Barbara (1842–
48).

1824–39 His first wife, Pauline Rousseau. A marriage of obligation. Michelet neglects Pauline, an ignorant woman, for his
work and his career. Pauline drinks. She dies of tuberculosis.
Michelet suffers regrets, remorse. He contemplates Pauline's body,
exhumed at Père-Lachaise. Two children from this marriage: Adèle,
who dies in 1855, and Charles, who dies in 1862.

1840–42 Madame Dumesnil, mother of Alfred, a student at
the Collège de France. A spiritual passion. Madame Dumesnil is
mortally ill. Michelet in despair at her death.

1848–74 His second wife, Athénaïs Mialaret. Michelet is fifty
when he sees, falls in love with, and marries this woman of twenty.
Athénaïs seeks to "inspire" the historian, to collaborate with him.
In this attempt she partially succeeds (in the works of natural his-
tory, but not in the history of France). After Michelet's death,
Athénaïs embarks on a career as abusive widow: she falsifies
Michelet's unpublished texts before turning them into dubious
posthumous works.

Michelet's daughter Adèle, bride of Alfred, Mme Dumesnil's son

Mme Dumesnil, *by Couture*

Athénaïs,
Michelet's second wife
by Armandine Parrot

Athénaïs Mialaret

Classic credo of the liberal petit-bourgeois around 1840:

—Modest conviction that the social classes will federate, but not disappear

—Pious hope of a cordial association between capital and labor

—Lamentations against mechanization

—Anticlericalism (Voltairean)

—Deism (Rousseauian)

—Infallibility of the People

—Béranger is the greatest poet of the age

—Germany (excepting Prussia) is a great country, generous and warmhearted

—Perfidious Albion

—France has two foes: priests and English gold

(1849) "The peculiar character of Social-Democracy is epitomized by the fact that democratic republican institutions are sought as a means not of doing away with capital and wage labor but of weakening their antagonism and transforming it into harmony . . . One must not form the narrow-minded notion that the petty bourgeoisie, on principle, wish to enforce an egoistic class interest. Rather, they believe that the *special* conditions of their emancipation are the *general* conditions within the frame of which alone modern society can be saved and the class struggle avoided. Just as little must one imagine that the democratic representatives are indeed all shopkeepers or enthusiastic champions of shopkeepers. According to their education and their individual position, they may be as far apart as heaven and earth. What makes them representatives of the petty bourgeoisie is the fact that in their minds they do not get beyond the limits which the latter do not get beyond in life, that they are consequently driven, theoretically, to the same problems and solutions to which material interest and social position drive the latter, practically. This is, in general, the relationship between the *political* and *literary representatives* of a class and the class they represent."—Marx, *The 18th Brumaire of Louis Bonaparte*

1819   Latin thesis *(De percipienda infinitate secundum Lockium)* and French thesis *(Examen des "Vies des hommes illustres" de Plutarque)*

1824   *Tableaux synchroniques de l'Histoire Moderne, 1453–1648*

1825   *Tableau chronologique de l'Histoire Moderne, 1453–1789*

1827   *Principe de la Philosophie de l'Histoire,* a free translation of Vico's *Principi d'una scienza nuova* (1 vol.)

1831   *Introduction à l'Histoire Universelle*
       Histoire romaine (2 vols.)

1833   *Précis de l'Histoire de France jusqu'à Révolution*

1835   A translation of Luther's memoirs
       An edition of selected works by Vico (2 vols.)

1837   *Origines du droit français*

1841   *Le procès des Templiers* (collection of documents, vol. 1)

1843   *Des Jésuites* (lectures at the Collège de France)

1845   *Du prêtre, de la femme, de la famille*

1846   *Le peuple*

1848   *L'Étudiant*

1850   *Le procès des Templiers* (vol. 2)

1851   *Légendes démocratiques du Nord*

1854   *Les femmes de la Révolution*
       Les soldats de la Révolution

1856   *L'oiseau*

1857   *L'insecte*

1858   *L'amour*

1859   *La femme*

1861   *La mer*

1862   *La sorcière*

1864   *La bible de l'humanité*

1868   *La montagne*

1869   *Nos fils*

1871   *La France devant l'Europe*

History of France
Moyen Age, 6 vols. (1833–44)

Révolution, 7 vols. (1847–53)
Temps Modernes, 7 vols. (1857–67)
Preface to the complete edition (1869)
Histoire du XIXe siècle, 3 vols. (1872–73)

Correspondence
Unpublished letters to Mlle Mialaret (Mme Michelet) (1899)
Unpublished letters, edited by Paul Sirven (1922)

Posthumous Works
Le banquet, ou un hiver en Italie
Ma jeunesse
Mon journal
Rome
Sur les chemins de l'Europe

Journal
Several fragments of Michelet's *Journal* were included by Gabriel
Monod in his two works on Michelet, but the *Journal intime* in its
entirety, bequeathed to the Institut by Michelet's widow, could not
be presented to the public before 1950. Publication began in 1959,
under the editorship of Paul Viallaneix: *Écrits de jeunesse* (*Journal
1820–23*), *Mémorial, Journal des idées; Journal* Vol. I (1828–48),
Journal Vol. II (1849–60).

Manuscripts
Michelet's remaining unpublished manuscripts are in the Biblio-
thèque historique de la Ville de Paris.

Complete Works
An edition of the Complete Works (20 vols.) is in progress, published by Flammarion, edited by Paul Viallaneix. Three volumes
have appeared: Vol. I (1798–1827); Vol. II (1828–31); Vol. III (1832–
38). Vols. IV–XI will contain the first critical edition of the *Histoire de France.*

CRITICAL BIBLIOGRAPHY

The following works on Michelet may be read with profit:
Eugène Noël, *Michelet et ses enfants* (Maurice Dreyfous, 1876)

Mme Edgar Quinet, *Cinquante ans d'amitié: Michelet et Quinet* (Armand Colin, 1899)

Gabriel Monod, *Jules Michelet* (Hachette, 1905)

Gabriel Monod, *La vie et la pensée de Jules Michelet* (Champion, 1923; 2 vols.)

Jean-Marie Carré, *Michelet et son temps* (Perrin, 1926)

Jean Guéhenno, *L'évangile éternel. Étude sur Michelet* (Grasset, 1927)

Daniel Halévy, *Jules Michelet* (Hachette, 1938)

Alfred Chabaud, *Jules Michelet* (Nouvelle Revue critique, 1919)

Gérard Walter, *Préface à l'Histoire de la Révolution* (Gallimard, Pléiade, 1939)

Lucien Febvre, *Michelet* (Les Classiques de la Liberté, Éd. des Trois Collines, Paris–Geneva, 1946

Oscar A. Haac, *Les principes inspirateurs de Michelet* (P.U.F., 1951)

Mary E. Johnson, *Michelet et le Christianisme* (Nizet, 1955)

P. Van Tieghem and J. Seebacher, *L'oeuvre de Michelet* (Hachette, 1956)

Jean Gaulmier, *Michelet* (collection "Les Écrivains devant Dieu," Desclée de Brouwer, 1968)

Paul Viallaneix, *La "Voie royale," essai sur l'idée du peuple dans l'oeuvre de Michelet* (Flammarion, 1971)

Works to Consult

Jean Pommier, *Les écrivains devant la Révolution de 1848* (P.U.F., 1948)

Roland Barthes, *Essais critiques* (Seuil, 1964)

Élie Faure, *Les constructeurs* (Gonthier, 1965)

Georges Poulet, *Mesure de l'instant* (Plon, 1968)

Michel Serres, *Hermès ou la communication* (Éd. de Minuit, 1968)

Alain Besançon, *Histoire et expérience du moi* (Flammarion, 1972)

Articles to Consult

Pierre Malandain, "Michelet et Napoléon, à travers les peintres de l'Empire," *Europe,* April–May 1969

Pierre Malandain, "Michelet et Géricault," *Revue d'histoire littéraire de la France,* Nov.–Dec. 1969

Paul Viallaneix, "Michelet devant Dieu," *Revue d'histoire littéraire de la France,* July–Aug. 1970

Gaëton Picon, "Michelet et la parole historienne," in *l'Étudiant* (Éd. du Seuil, 1970)

Jeanne Favret, "Sorcières et Lumières," *Critique,* April 1971

Paul Viallaneix, "Le héros selon Michelet," *Romantisme,* nos. 1–2 (1971)

Further References

L'Arc, no. 52, 1973: articles by Roland Barthes, Jacques Le Goff, Robert Mandrou, Claude Mettra, Pierre Nora, Paul Viallaneix, etc. This issue contains an important unpublished text by Michelet: "L'Héroïsme de l'esprit"

Catalogue de l'exposition Michelet, Archives de France, 1961, prepared by Jean-Pierre Babelon and Paul Viallaneix; 1 vol. of 160 pp.; 559 documents

Europe, Dec. 1973

TEXTS QUOTED

The texts quoted are from the following editions: *L'amour* (Calmann-Lévy, 1923); *Le banquet* (2nd ed., Calmann-Lévy, 1879); *La bible de l'humanité* (Calmann-Lévy, 1899); *La femme* (Calmann-Lévy, 1900); *Histoire de France: Moyen Age, Renaissance, Temps modernes* (Librairie internationale, 1871); *Introduction à l'Histoire Universelle* (Flammarion, Oeuvres complètes); *L'insecte* (Hachette, 1858); *La mer* (Calmann-Lévy); *La montagne* (Calmann-Lévy); *La sorcière* (Flammarion); *Le peuple* (Calmann-Lévy, 1877); *Histoire de la Révolution et Histoire du XIXe siècle* (Calmann-Lévy, 1899)

The titles of the selections are not Michelet's.

Michelet in 1834
Medallion by David d'Angers

MICHELET, EATER OF HISTORY

"Men of letters always suffer, and live no less for that."
—*Michelet to Eugène Noël*

MIGRAINES   *Michelet's disease is the migraine, that mixture of vertigo and nausea. For him, everything brings on migraine: cold, storms, springtime, wind, the History he is writing. This man, who produced an encyclopedic oeuvre of sixty volumes, inveterately declares himself "dizzy, sickly, empty-headed, weak." He writes constantly (during fifty-six years of his adult life) yet is always in a state of total collapse. Major events in this life: oppressive storms, releasing rains, returning autumns. Nor does Michelet relent in his demands on a body overcome by an inopportune draft: whenever he can, he travels from region to region, alert to unfavorable conditions of wind and sun, changing residence a hundred times accordingly.*

Dying repeatedly, and believing each crisis is the last, he is reborn all the more delightedly. Consider him at forty-four: he feels he is entering "that long torment, old age"; but consider him once again six years later, at fifty: he is about to marry a woman of twenty and cheerfully embark on a third life. Nor is this all: after Woman, the Elements; Michelet is yet to experience three great rebirths: Earth (mud baths at Acqui, near Turin); Water (his first sea bathing, at fifty); Sun (at Hyères).

WORK   *All of which, interrupted by his customary sickliness, fits of nausea, makes for a body vulnerable to and parasitical upon the most arbitrary powers. Yet, in truth, this disjointed physiology seems accessible only to the most brutal constraint of all: work. In the very periods he believed himself threatened by every possible dispersion of the body—i.e., throughout his whole life—this man was possessed by an insensate rage to work. Schedules (draconian), results (vast output), even egoism (which leads him to forsake his first wife and abandon his dying son)— all testify to the fact. Yet this frenzied labor (of inquiry, of erudition, and of writing), governed by a virtually monastic discipline, inveterately sustained its prophetic tension. Routinized in form, it was maintained at a constant tragic pitch.*

Here then is what his migraines could offer Michelet: creation as a responsible choice. Jeopardized by a storm or a spring, his oeuvre becomes a gesture significant at every moment. To fecundate an existence perceived as empty and weak by the virile value of impassioned work is to bestow upon the fruits of that work a kind of superlative signification—of prophetic character. It would be little enough to say that for Michelet work was a form of hygiene: one would have to call it dietetic; Michelet is a dead man when he is not at work—how many times he remarks on just this subject!—hence everything in him is prepared to constitute history as a nutriment. Michelet organizes his physical weakness as a parasite would do, i.e., he burrows into the heart of historical substance, feeds on it, grows in it, and though existing only by its means, triumphantly invades it.

THE VICTIM OF HISTORY   *Work—in other words, History—being a nutritive habitat in which every weakness is certain of being a value, migraines are here transferred, i.e., rescued, endowed with signification. Michelet's whole body becomes the product of his own creation, and a kind of surprising symbiosis is established between the historian and History. Fits of nausea, dizziness, oppression do not come only from the seasons,* from the weather; it is the very horror of narrated history which provokes them: Michelet has "historical" migraines. We are not to regard this as a metaphor, they are real migraines: September 1792, the beginnings of the Convention, the Terror, so many immediate diseases, concrete as toothaches. Michelet is always said to have an excessive sensibility; yes, but above all a sensibility concerted, inflected, directed toward a signification. To be the victim of History is to constitute History not only as a nutriment and as a sacred poison but also as a possessed object; "historical" migraines have no purpose but to establish Michelet as the manducator, priest, and owner of History.*

It is not only the god's substance that enters the priest's body by a ritual manducation, it is also the god's death. Michelet afflicts himself with the most terrible historical diseases, he takes them on himself, he dies of History the way one dies—or rather the way one does not die—of love. "I have drunk too deep of the black blood of the dead"—this means that, with each migraine, Michelet renews in himself the death of the People-as-god, of History-as-god. But at the same time this death survived and repeated acts as a nutriment, for it is this death which constitutes Michelet as a historian, makes him into a pontiff who absorbs, sacrifices, bears witness, fulfills, glorifies.†

J'AI HÂTE And the Christological theme persists: Michelet receives History as a nutriment, but in return he abandons his life to it: not only his work and his health, but even his death. In fact, Michelet places his own time, by a kind of trigonometric reduction, beneath the very extent of the ages and advances toward his death with a movement proportional to that by which his History hastens toward its conclusion: when death threatens,

*We are of course concerned here with an unconscious intentionality; it would be meaningless—and futile—to question Michelet's sincerity.
† To glorify is to manifest in essence . . .

History can only make haste. But when does death threaten? No one knows for certain. Michelet is quite familiar with the omega of History (the Revolution), but he cannot foresee if he will have the time necessary to conduct the celebration of History to its conclusion. Whence the haste mingled with anguish, and that frenzied movement which precipitates the History of France, as the age of death approaches. The longer Michelet lives, the more he blazes up, devoured by the necessity to consummate History as far ahead as possible. The whole end of his life is thereby placed under the device of the Dukes of Burgundy (which he so often quotes with enjoyment): J'ai hâte [I make haste].

In this regard, the great preface of 1869, which marks the victorious closure of the Histoire de France *(23 volumes, 36 years, 20 centuries), echoes with the solemnity of an* Ite, missa est. *The two time spans overlap, and, the Revolution at last consummated, joined to the centuries which have prepared it, the historian can die. Which is what Michelet will do, not without suffering—cruelly, it would appear—a reprieve of five years he does not know what to do with: five tragically useless years— worse still: unintelligible years, which he can only fill with one long cry of bitterness, fiercely protesting, in his last three books (the* Histoire de la XIXe siècle *and its apocalyptic preface), that History is over and that he is merely the last man in a machine-world.*

MICHELET THE WALKER *How does Michelet eat History? He "grazes" on it; i.e., he passes over it and at the same time he swallows it. The corporeal gesture which best accounts for this double operation is* walking; *also, we must remember that, for the romantics, travel had an entirely different effect from its modern counterpart; nowadays we participate in a journey by "eyes only," and the very rapidity of our course makes whatever we see a kind of remote and motionless screen. The*

Michelet in 1842
Drawing by Couture

physiology of romantic travel (walking or coach) is just the contrary: here, landscape is slowly, arduously conquered; landscape surrounds, presses in, threatens, invades—one must force one's way through it, and not only by eyes but by muscles and patience: whence its beauty and its terrors, which today seem to us excessive: romantic travel knows two movements in which the human body is engaged: either the discomfort of progress or else the euphoria of a panorama.

MICHELET THE SWIMMER   *This double apprehension is the whole of Michelet's History. Of course, the most numerous moments are the discomfort, the fatigue of a forced march through a grim historical region of petty and faded motives, one that is in fact too close to the historian-traveler. This is what Michelet calls "rowing" ("I am rowing through Louis XI. I am rowing through Louis XIV. I swim laboriously. I am rowing vigorously through Richelieu and the Fronde"). Yet the plunge involves an incomplete assimilation of History, a failed nutrition, as if the body, thrust into an element where it does not breathe, found itself stifled by the very proximity of space.*

OVERVIEW   *The ideal nutrition is the kind proposed by what was known as the* tableau. *Historical* tableaux *(for example, Flanders in the fifteenth century) are frequent in Michelet, and they always furnish a euphoria, for they relieve, they suspend both fatigue and ignorance, they afford rest, breath, and a view. Contrary to the narrative, which reduces the historian's body to the rank of an object, the* tableau *(the overview) placed Michelet virtually in God's position, for God's chief power is precisely to hold in a simultaneous perception moments, events, men, and causes which are humanly dispersed through time, space, or different orders. The* tableau *takes the place of the ancient cosmogonies: in both cases, human history is perceived as creation (in the one case, divine; in the other, Micheletist), i.e., as an object whose Maker is outside, actually above, located on a different level, from which he gazes without being seen.*

To write History is therefore, for Michelet, to follow a destined itinerary which affords him one askesis *after another, a series of felicities, and, according to the progress-on-foot or the rest from it, makes him a suffering god or a triumphant one. Narrative is calvary, the* tableau *is glory, but of course between these two movements there is a relation of tension; Micheletist history proceeds by waves: the narrative is always conducted toward a display, an epiphany, and the* tableau *is never closed, its goal is an anxiety, the historian's reprise of a humbled incarnation, that of the breathless rower or, one might say, of the god returned to his Passion. Again, no chapter of Michelet is ever really conclusive, but no line of facts is ever without its tropism. Everything is linked together, not by virtue of a rhetorical plan, but by that kind of existential* tempo *which makes Michelet the traveler, then the spectator; the eater, then the ruminant of History.*

Consider how he progresses in his fourteenth century (by erudition, above all); he advances, he narrates, he adds the years to the years, the facts to the facts, in short he rows, blind and stubborn as a long-distance swimmer; and then, all of a sudden, without any warning, *he encounters the figure of the peasant Jacques, standing on his plowed field: profound astonishment, even trauma, then emotion, euphoria of the traveler who, caught short, stops, sees, and understands; a second level of history, this one entirely panoramic, consisting of intellection, is revealed: the historian shifts, for a while, from labor to Festivity.*

MICHELET THE PREDATOR *Michelet's discourse—what is usually called his style—is precisely that kind of concerted navigation which brings side by side, like a shark and its prey, History and its narrator. Michelet is one of those predatory writ-*

ers (Pascal, Rimbaud) who cannot write without constantly devouring their discourse. This voration consists for Michelet in substituting for the oratorical cadence of noble art certain abrupt interpolations, certain peremptory remarks such as "Let us say," "You will have," "I shall return to this," "I suppose," "I should say," "It must be said" . . . And the preface, the note, or the postface are to the discourse what the interpolation is to the sentence: these recurrent glances of Michelet's into his work are frequent (what Proust called, apropos of Michelet himself, his musician's cadences).

No relation between this kind of interruption and the old "subjectivity" of school manuals. It would make more sense to contrast "sliding" writers of the Chateaubriand sort, whom Michelet held in the greatest horror, to devouring writers of the Michelet sort. The former spread their discourse, accompany it without interrupting it, and gradually maneuver the sentence toward a final euphoria; they are writers with rules and formulas. The latter, on the contrary, threatened with losing their prey if they preen too much, constantly interlard their speech with unfinished gestures, like the obsessive movements of an owner who swiftly reassures himself of the presence of his property; for them, there is no final cadence, no display, no horizontal slide of the writer alongside his sentence, but a series of brief, frequent plunges, breaks in the rhetorical euphoria, in short, what Sainte-Beuve has splendidly called Michelet's vertical style. Chateaubriand's sentence always ends in décor, it hears itself sliding to its close; Michelet's swallows itself—destroys itself.

This suicide is intentional. Michelet feared art precisely to the degree that he had a gift for it; as we know, he wrote quite spontaneously in verse, and felt himself to be constantly pursued by "style." Now, art—let us say, traditional rhetoric, with its rules and formulas, like that of the frère ennemi, Chateaubriand—art is an obstacle to the nutritive exchanges between historian and History. Art is an isolator ("Art besmirches me like a coat of varnish, so that whatever happens to me, good or bad, enters me like the acid in engravings, and etches just deeply enough for a work of art"), it keeps two organisms from uniting and mutually fortifying each other: the historian can no longer eat History, but only gaze at it and slide over it, as along a smooth, shiny, and sterile film. Art puts history on show and makes the historian into a writer. A doom that Michelet had the greatest difficulty avoiding. We know that, in the best of cases, posterity has managed to save Michelet only by embalming him in the folds of a purely stylistic anthology (purple passages and graduation speeches: the Tableau of France, Jeanne d'Arc, the swallow, the jellyfish, etc.).

HISTORY-AS-OBJECT   Of course, History for Michelet could be a ritual aliment only because he posited it in its total extension, granting himself the power of communicating by daily manducation with a History-as-God, and not with a History-as-Science. Neither Michelet's migraines nor his walk across narrative nor his broken style would have had a ritual meaning if Michelet had been only the historian of one period (like Thiers, Barante, or Lamartine). The encyclopedic character of a work which apprehends not only all ages, from the age of reptiles down to Waterloo, but also every possible order of historical object, from the invention of infantry to the nursing of the British baby, participates in Michelet's humanity to the same degree as his migraines or his prefaces. For History can be the object of an appropriation only if it is constituted as an authentic object, supplied with two ends or poles. History can be an aliment only when it is full as an egg; hence Michelet has filled his, has endowed it with two goals and one direction: his History has actually become a philosophy of History. History is to be consummated, i.e., on the one hand, concluded, fulfilled, and, on the other, consumed, devoured, ingested, so as to resuscitate the historian.

Michelet, *by Belloc*

THE DUTCH CANALBOAT

For Michelet, the Dutch canalboat is the ideal site of the family. This concave, full object, this egglike, solid space suspended in the smooth element of the waters, constantly exchanging the moisture of ablutions and the liquidity of the atmosphere, is the delicious image of the homogeneous. Here the great Micheletist theme is posited: that of a seamless world.

THE SMOOTH   *Consider, for example, the King of France in the Middle Ages: his power derives from his empty space, in other words from his "smoothness," from that sort of superior state where a thousand forces, a thousand heredities cancel each other out in him, releasing a general and delectable non-signification from the accidental. Contrasted to the King of England—bloodthirsty, proud, "private"—his very weakness erases his limits, he shares the same skin with the rest of his universe: ideally, he is nothing but a void, a humility thrust into the ermine robe, but drawing everything else into itself: the people, the bourgeoisie, the Church. The same ideality is posited for France in Europe, and for the Center in France: they have the higher plenitude, that of the innumerable, they are neutral and smooth as an empty space, and they reveal, like certain animals, a real aptitude for procrypsis, for the infinite plasticity of superficial characteristics.*

PROSE   *One element summarizes all the qualities of the non-signifying, and that is Prose. The King of France is prosaic, central France is prosaic, i.e., in them a general form unifies the particularity of movements and origins. Here we must remember that the Prose / Poetry pairing greatly disturbed the eighteenth century; the Franco-British* Aufklärer *believed prose to be posterior to poetry; the world had first spoken in verse, which in a progressist view of History gave prose a higher value, since it was the language of a more developed civilization. For Michelet, Prose is a sign of the homogeneous, and it is as such that it is a value, fruit of a grace or of a conquest. We have seen how he himself was threatened by Poetry as by a natal inferno, and aspired to Prose as to a decisive liberation, one which would allow him to devour History and to unite with it.*

UNION–UNITY   *Prose is superior, insofar as it is the absence of individual characteristics, the product of a fusion and not of a collection: in the medieval king, in central France, all seams are erased, there no longer remains the trace of any origin, of any feature, of any individuality—there is a void, hence perfect smoothness. Prose being the product of an erasure, we must give this erasure a moral name: it is unity. Unity has a doubly imperfect version: union. Union is an inferior state because it merely compounds positive elements which it can harmonize but not abolish. Unity is superior to it, insofar as it destroys the very memory of the constitutive individualities and elicits in their place a zone of absence, in which everything is once again possible, presented to the incubation of cordial warmth: this is freedom. History has not failed to present numerous phenomena of union: states have been united, races harmonized. But there has never been but one unity, that of France, and in France, that of the Federations of '90.*

The Federations are the central action of the Revolution ("the finest day of my life," Michelet says), because the integration of France was achieved on that day, not by a simple addition of provinces (union), but by a veritable phenomenon of chemical concretion (unity), which has destroyed all the constituent pieces, leaving in their place only a unanimous warmth, the smooth, warm air of a new plenitude: la patrie. *Nor does this chemical operation (we must not forget that Lavoisier is still quite close to Michelet) lack a reactive presence: the religious counterrevolution which tried to attack the federative synthesis, in the manner of a decomposing substance.*

The Tableau of France *itself, which is ordinarily presented as the ancestor of geographies, is in fact the account of a chemical experiment: its enumeration of the provinces is less a description than a methodical list of the materials, the substances necessary to the chemical elaboration of French generality. One might say it is something like the nomenclature put at the head of a good recipe: take a little Champagne, a little Picardie, a little Normandie, Anjou, and Beauce, stir them around a central core, the Ile-de-France, steep them in this negative pole, and you will have the superlative nation of Europe: France. This is what Michelet has done; once the elements are enumerated, described, weighed, judged, he has posited the principle of their mixture: thanks to that very special polarity which has surrounded the negative center of France with a belt of marches, i.e., of positive (hence incomplete) Frances, France is merely an infinite chemical action, it exists only in that void sustained by the very arrangement of its parts. And this is a privilege which only France possesses. England and Germany, for example, are lacking in polarity: England is only a hard, substantial plenitude (English grass, English mutton, English blood, English gold), i.e., un-*

suited to the beneficent chemistry of the void; Germany is only a mass without future and without history, without limits and without rotundity (water, sand, the Ghibelline spirit, deprived of the formative power of the Law).

ACTION   Thus, Michelet's notion of the homogeneous is furnished with a very specific means of fabrication: mixture. The young Michelet had inherited two schemas: History-as-Plant (Herder), and History-as-Spiral (Vico). In the Introduction à l'Histoire Universelle (1831), he adds the image of History-as-Synthesis. A dawning chemistry and transformism have given it to him: a decisive image, for it permitted Michelet to choose the homogeneous as an action and not as a state. A theme, ambiguous as always in Michelet, i.e., at once vitalist and moralistic, accounts for this: action. This superlatively beneficent theme, and one which Michelet has apposed as an index of value to certain privileged historical objects (France, the eighteenth century, Frederick the Great, Leibniz), is none other, in a moralizing form, than the schema of the chemical amalgam of bodies or of the natural mixture of species. It is a figure of great novelty, since it substitutes for the image of a universe collated and composed (Newton) that of a universe which is continuous because it ceaselessly creates itself. A new schema, that of continuity ("Life grows uno tenore"), takes the place of the old classical order.

In fact, Michelet continued to militate in favor of Geoffroy Saint-Hilaire, the transformist, against Cuvier, the creationist; in favor of Lavoisier, the chemist, against Laplace, the mathematician. Mathematics, momentarily rescued thanks to the beneficent theme of the golden number of the Italian thinker-architects (Dante, Vico, Brunelleschi), ultimately fell under the general suspicion attached to a "constructed" and not "grown" universe. Michelet made Napoleon into a (false) mathematician,

The Sword and the Principle: Frederick the Great
"This was the most complete character of the eighteenth century, being the only one to unite idea with power." —*Histoire de France*

thereby mutually discrediting the tyrant and his science, that of the "popes" Laplace and Cuvier.

Transformism: a bulwark of the Micheletist notion of the homogeneous. It is not only in his naturalist works but in his History itself that Michelet consistently applies the Lamarckian figure of the scala viventium, *the gradual ladder of living beings. Many philosophies, in that eighteenth century on which Michelet was chiefly brought up, prepared the design of a universe outspread like a great animal organism: Leibniz, a Micheletist hero ("Marble has ideas, however confused"), Bonnet, and Robinet (beings are linked in a chain, from atom to cherub), and even more certainly the Gnostics (Restif, Mesmer, Fabre d'Olivet, Lavater, and Saint-Martin). Michelet could find no better language for his project of plenitude than this smooth display of forms melting into one another, gradually advancing from equation to equation so that the final term becomes a kind of metaphor of the initial form and there is no longer any essential difference between beings and objects, the realms of nature and moral ideas.*

ITINERANT SUBSTANCE   *Michelet describes with relish all the intermediary states of matter, savoring these ambiguous zones of process in which flint gives way to grain, then to the Frenchman whom it nourishes; in which plant extends to animal, fish to mammal, swan to woman (the Renaissance Leda), Jew to pebble, billy goat to prophet (Michelangelo's Moses); in which the baby's brain is nothing but the milky flower of the camellia; in which man himself can be substituted for woman in the transhumance of marriage. Does not the tree extend beyond its order? Yes, it groans, weeps, and is filled with a vegetal dream. The most obdurate substance, stone itself, is transformed just like a Lamarckian species; stones are alive, according to the old medieval expression* (vide *the cathedral builder,* magister de vivis lapidibus): *the ogive, for example, proceeds from hole to heart, then to flame.*

WATER-AS-FISH   *Now, to describe these transitions is like caressing them. To proceed from soft, viscous water, neither fluid nor formed, to transparent fish* which appear to be generated by it is to discern an absence of seam and to proclaim this ideal smoothness. Thus, in that instability of matter so delicious to Michelet, one substance is privileged: water. Water can support the thousand intermediary states of matter: the clear, the crystalline, the transparent, the fleeting, the gelatinous, the viscous, the whitish, the swarming, the rounded, the elastic—all dialectics are possible between water and man. But this is not all: by its linking power, water is also the mythic element of fecundations, i.e., the homogeneity it proposes is space-as-duration, at once substance and future.† Michelet often speaks of the world-as-fish, and always associates it with the world-as-Woman. These two worlds are for him those of spontaneous generation (in which he firmly believed) and of parthenogenesis. It is understood that water is the archetype of all links and connections, and that here the homogeneous intensifies, it produces life: water engenders skin, it is actually and ultimately the same surface.*

GOETHE-AS-DOG   *No barrier of essence between the orders of nature: the mineral is the plant, the animal contains the human dream. Consider the beasts: "Do they not seem to be children whose development has been forbidden by a wicked fairy and who have not been able to disentangle the first dream of the cradle? . . . A sad enchantment, in which the captive being of an imperfect thing depends on all those surrounding it, like a person asleep."‡ The elephant, by its exemplary gentleness, is*

---

*Procrypsis of pelagic creatures in seawater is a Darwinian principle.
†On the genetic power of the Fish, see Montesquieu, *Esprit des lois* (XXIII, 13).
‡We shall see later on how Michelet dreaded the theme of drowsiness. This terror of "sleeping" must be contrasted with the enthusiasm for shadows, night, closed eyes, and folded arms in Proust and Valéry, for instance.

perhaps a former Brahman; even at the very bottom of the animal scale, the jellyfish is merely "the dream of a destiny impossible to achieve," and Michelet's dogs, Zémire and Mirza, remind him (with dread and remorse) of his first wife, Pauline: what if they were she? Goethe loathed dogs, fearing that his monad might be absorbed in them.

SUSPENDED STATES   *This indeterminacy of matter and of its states could ultimately absorb Michelet's very body: the migraines and fits of nausea, the seizures and bouts of dizziness predispose him, moreover, to the unfolding of the body. At Acqui, Michelet takes a mud bath, he exchanges his body with the Earth and observes all the phases of this transubstantiation: here he becomes depersonalized, linked to the sand: no seams between himself and the universe; in his marble tub—his coffin, he says— he is confined, full and mingled as in the ideal Dutch canalboat, closed like a womb. At Toulon, another identity: early in the morning, seeing the dawn break almost reluctantly, he enjoys a delicious difficulty in being weaned from Night, in remaining suspended in that ideal paradox: the dawn, i.e., the very essence of the transitory.*

Thus, the sciences of the period (Lavoisier and Geoffroy), then metempsychosis (vulgarized by the Hinduists Burnouf and Anquetil, adapted by Michelet's friends Pierre Leroux and Jean Raynaud), finally the psychology of a Maine de Biran—all this affords Michelet the beneficent movement of an outspread universe. Nature is no longer a catalogue, as with the Encyclopedists, but a surface: take a pinch of canvas and everything comes, the world is smooth as silk.

Yet one question remains: What becomes of this homogeneity when one shifts from the level of Nature to that of History? What is the homogeneous in time?

[34]

HISTORY-AS-PLANT *Here, too, it is the sciences of Nature which afford an answer. History grows* "uno tenore," *like a plant or a species, its movement is less a succession than a continuity. Are there, strictly speaking, historical facts? No; history is rather a continuity of identities, just as the plant or the species is the extension of one and the same tissue. As we have seen, moreover, Michelet advances into History like a swimmer through the water, History surrounds him like a solution. Except that the* tableau *has a visual, hence comparative, hence logical function. All the rest of history is walking, i.e., muscular existence, uneasy hence strong apprehension of a continuity.*

NO CAUSALITY *The vegetal character of historic growth obviously excludes causality. Michelet has nothing to do with an order of explanation which would set in opposition such heterogeneous objects as cause and effect. Who would even think of saying that the jellyfish is "cause" of the whale, or even that the seed is "cause" of the flower? No, they are simply two more or less remote zones of the same substance. The same goes for the objects of history: some are not the causes of others, they are merely the different moments of the same stem.*

There exists a certain type of Micheletist causality, but it remains discreetly relegated to the unlikely realms of morality. These are "necessities" of a moral order, entirely psychological postulates, which have the power elsewhere assigned to mechanical causes. For instance: spontaneous generation must exist, because it would be an impiety not to believe in it; Greece cannot have been homosexual, because Greece is all light; Frederick the Great must not have been a pederast, because he had "a powerful soul and nerves of steel"; the family must not exist in

France, because the family is characteristic of Protestant countries.*

HISTORY-AS-EQUATION   *Evidently, we are concerned here with a purely static causality; moreover, History does not advance by causes but by equalities. From the peasant Jacques to Jeanne d'Arc, the succession is not of causal but of equational order. Jeanne is not the result of a certain number of antecedent data. She is essentially a relay of identities: she equals both the People and the Revolution, rather as the flower "represents" the primal seed and the future fruit, or as the whale is an identity common to both Fish and Woman. In this way, there is equation but not causal progression between Louis the Meek, Robert the Pious, Godefroy de Bouillon, Thomas Becket, and Jeanne d'Arc: all are weak, all are Christ, all are the People.*†

POSTPONED EQUALITIES   *Naturally, these equalities can be more or less delayed. Certain essences of the Revolution, for example, are lodged quite far back in time. Others offer unexpected ramifications: in the first period of the Middle Ages, until Philip the Fair, the King of France is identified with the People by the relay of a third equational term: the Church. But, whatever the detours, History remains homogeneous, and the chain of identities which constitutes it possesses for Michelet a major nutritive power: familiarity. Since History is merely a continuity of identical objects, the historian is never lost within it, he* recognizes *all its figures at the moment they offer themselves to*

*Faguet had discerned this inverted characteristic of Micheletist causality *(Dix-neuvième siècle)*.
†It is this progression by identities which Hegel condemned as tautology; without knowing him well, Michelet could not endure Hegel, whom he discredited in his way by linking him to the malefic theme of the Fatal and the Mechanical, i.e., dry Death.

him. As we have seen, Michelet was at first surprised to encounter Jacques; but a moment was enough for him to recognize, in this brutal peasant, the very essence of the People. And just as the fiber "explains" the plant, as the cell "explains" the animal, so there is a principial substance common to all historical landscapes: this is what Michelet calls the eternal Gospel.* The notion of the eternal Gospel is itself nothing but Lamarckian transformism applied to Christianity: Justice is the basis of all moments of history—including the Christian moment—and history is merely the equational sequence of its figures.

In a sense, the perennial nature of the moral essence restores Micheletist History to a para-mathematical order: history progresses by transformations (in Condillac's sense of the term) more than by evolutions. The distinction has its significance on the level of ideas, not on that of existence. For what Michelet chooses is the movement *of continuity, not its structure; whence an intellectual but not an existential ambiguity.*

WILL-TO-LIVE *Yet these identities require the appearance of displacement. How does one shift from one figure of the Just Man to the next? The motor principle will once again be the same for Nature and for History. Vital for the one, moral for the other, in both cases what is involved is a will-to-live. The jellyfish hastens toward a more evolved form of animality by the same movement with which primitive India anticipates and aspires to the Revolution of '89.*

But here there is no naturalism of morality: it is not the natural realm which affords morality its movement, but just the converse: Nature progresses from realm to realm according to

*"The Vaudois, disengaging the Gospel from place and time, teach that it is renewed every day, that the incarnation of God in man ceaselessly begins again and that it is His passion. Hence the Gospel does not date from a certain year of the reign of Tiberius; it is of all times; it is the Eternal Gospel."

the paths of a veritable civic emancipation. Michelet does not naturalize morality, he moralizes Nature. The important thing is that these realms meet, and that in the universe nothing is ever alone, stripped of its double. It is ultimately Micheletist morality—i.e., everything that to us seems to proceed from an improbable rhetoric—which constitutes History as a delicious, indeed an essential unctuosity, since it is in the warmth of this closed, full History that Michelet will deposit, as an intelligent parasite, his own organism.

France is the country of prose. What are all the prose writers of the world beside Bossuet, Pascal, Montesquieu, and Voltaire? Now, prose is of all forms of writing the least figurative and the least concrete, the most abstract, the most transparent, the purest; in other words, the least material, the freest, the most common to all men, the most *human*. Prose is the last form of thought, what is furthest from the vague and inactive reverie, what is closest to action. The passage from mute symbolism to poetry, from poetry to prose, is a progress toward the equality of minds; it is an intellectual leveling. Hence, from the mysterious hierarchy of Oriental castes emerges the heroic aristocracy; from the latter, the modern democracy. The democratic genius of our nation appears nowhere more clearly than in its eminently prosaic character, and it is indeed in that character that it is destined to raise the whole world of intelligences to equality.

1831. *Introduction à l'Histoire Universelle*

PLANT OR ANIMAL?

"Our earthly fields and forests," Darwin tells us, "would seem naked deserts if compared to those of the sea." And,

Michelet in 1847

indeed, all those who venture upon the transparent seas of the Indies are struck by the phantasmagoria which the depths afford, one chiefly astonishing by the singular exchanges made by plants and animals of their natural insignia, of their appearance. The soft and gelatinous plants, with rounded organs which seem neither stems nor leaves, affecting the fleshiness, the softness of animal curves, appear to want us to be deceived, to believe them to be animals. The authentic animals look as if they were striving to be plants and to resemble the vegetable realm. They imitate everything in that other kingdom: some have the solidity, the quasi-eternity of trees; others blossom and then fade, even as flowers. Thus, the sea anemone opens as a pale pink daisy, or as a garnet aster embellished with azure eyes. But once its corolla has released a daughter, a new anemone, you will see it collapse and faint away.

1861. La mer, II, 3.

WATER OR FISH?

Seawater, even the purest, sampled in mid-ocean, far from any admixture, is whitish and rather viscous. Pressed between the fingers, it forms *threads,* and slowly drips away. Chemical analyses do not account for this characteristic. There is an organic substance here which such analyses attain only by destroying, depriving it of its particularity, and brutally restoring it to the general elements.

The plants and creatures of the sea are dressed in this substance, whose mucosity, consolidated around them, has a gelatinous effect, sometimes fixed and sometimes tremulous: they gleam through it as through a diaphanous garment. And nothing adds more to the fantastic illusions which the world of the seas affords us. Their reflections are singular, often strangely iridescent—on the scales of fish, for instance, or on the molluscs which seem to derive from it the entire splendor of their nacreous shells.

This is what most attracts the child who sees a fish for the first time. I was very young when this happened to me, but I perfectly recall the intense impression. This brilliant, flashing creature, clad in its silver scales, cast me into amazement, inexpressible delight. I tried to capture it, but found it as difficult to catch hold of as the water that ran through my tiny fingers. It seemed to me identical with the element in which it swam. I had the vague notion that it was nothing but water, animal or animate water, organized water.

Much later, having grown up, I was scarcely less amazed when I examined, on a beach, one of the Radiata. Through its transparent body, I could make out the individual grains of sand. Colorless as glass, barely substantial, shivering when touched, it looked to me as it did to the ancients and even to Réaumur, who simply called such creatures *gelatinized water.*

How much more powerful such an impression becomes when one finds in their initial formation the yellowish-white ribbons wherein the sea produces a soft sketch of its solid fucus, the laminaria which, turning brown, attain to the solidity of leather hides. But still quite young, in the viscous state, in their elasticity, they have something of the consistency of a solidified wave, all the stronger for being softer.

1861. *La mer,* II, 2

THE MASTER OF LIVING STONES

At Pentecost, white pigeons were released in the church among tongues of flame, flowers rained down, the inner galleries were illuminated. At other festivals, the illumination was outside. Imagine the effect of the lights on these prodigious monuments, when the clergy, gliding along the upper ramps, animated the shadowy masses with their fantastic processions, passing in their rich vestments back and forth along the balustrades, those lacy bridges, holding candles and chanting; when lights and voices revolved in circle after circle, and down below, in the shadows, the ocean of people responded. Here, for this age, was the true drama, the true mystery, the representation of humanity's journey through the three worlds, that sublime intuition which Dante received from fugitive reality only to seize and eternalize it in the *Divina Commedia*.

This colossal theater of the sacred drama has returned, after its long medieval festivity, to silence and darkness. The faint voice one hears in it, that of the priest, is powerless to fill the vaults, whose size was created to include and contain the thunder of the people's voices. The place is widowed, the church is empty. Its profound symbolism, which spoke so loud in those days, has gone mute. Now it is an object of scientific curiosity, of philosophical explanations of Alexandrine interpretations. The church is a Gothic museum visited by the learned: they circulate through it, stare at it without reverence, and praise instead of praying. Do they even know what it is they are praising? What finds favor in their eyes, what pleases them in the church, is not the church itself; it will be the delicate labor of its ornaments, the fringe of its mantle, its stone lace, a certain subtle and laborious work of the Gothic style in its decadence.

There is something great here, whatever the fate of a religion. The future of Christianity has nothing to do with it. Let us touch these stones cautiously, let us walk lightly on these slabs. A great mystery has taken place here. Now I see nothing but death, and I am tempted to weep. The Middle Ages, the French Middle Ages, have expressed in architecture their innermost thoughts: the cathedrals of Paris, of Saint-Denis, of Rheims, say more about their times than the longest narratives. The stone is animated and spiritualized beneath the artist's severe and ardent hands: out of them wells up life. The artist is well named in the Middle Ages: the master of living stones, *magister de vivis lapidibus.*

1861. *Histoire de France,* II, *Éclaircissements*

FLAMES, HEARTS, TEARS

Consider the deep, narrow orbit of the Gothic arch, of that *ogival eye,* when it strives to open, in the twelfth century. This eye of the Gothic arch is the sign by which the new architecture achieves its identity. The old art, worshipper of substance, was identified by the temple's material support, by the column, whether Tuscan, Doric, or Ionic. Modern art, child of the soul and the mind, has for its principle not form but physiognomy—the eye; not the column but the vault; not the full but the empty. In the twelfth and thirteenth centuries, the vault thrust into the very thickness of the walls, like the solitary of the Thebaid in a granite cave, is entirely withdrawn into itself; it meditates and dreams. Gradually it advances toward the outside, it reaches the external surface of the wall. It radiates at last into lovely mystic roses, triumphant with celestial glory. But the fourteenth century has no sooner passed than these roses change; they are transformed into flamboyant figures; are they flames, hearts, or tears?

Ibid.

PEBBLE-MEN, FISH-MEN

In the conscientious paintings of the Egyptians, striking in their lifelike truth, one may see what were, seventeen centuries before Christ, the Syrian, the Assyrian, the Arab or the Jew, the Negro, the European (apparently, the Greek). True masterpieces. The Greek, who might have been painted today, is the island mariner, with his hard, delicate profile, his piercing eye. The Negroes are extraordinarily lifelike: in their excessive and ungainly gesticulation, it has been clearly noted that they are not stupid, but excessively active, their blood too rich, their minds distracted, carried away, half mad. This is exactly the opposite of the Bedouin dryness, of the lean Arab who is not without nobility, of the Jew's harsh aridity. The latter, Sinai pebbles cut with a sharp razor, will live, will endure, I am convinced. But the bastard figures of Babel and Phoenicia do not seem viable: they are ephemerae which would survive only as species, like the insects by an incessant renewal of the generations. —The man of the Euphrates is a fish. —The man of Tyre, a batrachian. —In the man of Babel, the receding forehead and the backward cranial development belong to the aquatic world. They remind us of his god (the Fish Magus). Yet this man is not at all disagreeable, or lacking in a certain grace of movement. He seems loose and ready: he appears to be saying "welcome" to you. One readily understands that the peoples and gods dissolved into one another in Babylon, lost in such confusion. The others, whom I believe to be Phoenicians, are not, like these Babylonians, swathed in fine gowns. They are, as sailors, ready for action, with bare arms, in short tunics which do not hamper their actions. Their gaze is that of people who always see far off, across the wide plains of the sea. The faces, handsome and grave yet strange, are astonishing: they have no necks. Strangely misshapen, they have suffered, from precocious vices, an arrested development. On their countenance, there is a cold cruelty which must abet them in their dreadful trade, their raids on human flesh.

1864. *La bible de l'humanité,* II, 2

In a lively foam of the viscous, sticky water which ferments and seethes, in the swarming sea, Syria has received its god. Like the Euphrates, its ideal was the fish, and the Woman-as-Fish.

Of course, if the infinity of an inferior form of love, of fecundation, appears anywhere, it is in the fish! It would swell the seas. Would literally drown the waters, at certain times, whitening them, illuminating them with another sea of milk, greasy, thick, and phosphorescent.

Here is the Venus of Syria, Derceto, Astarte or Astaroth, male and female both, the dream of generation. The Hebrew, at the edges of the desert, with his harsh life, dreams of a nation numerous as the swirling sands. The Phoenician, in his malodorous harbor cities, dreams of the infinity of the tides, a nation of amphibia which swarm and are cast up from Sidon to Carthage and to the very shores of Ocean.

Inland, for the amorous Syrian woman, the cooing, lascivious race of countless doves, a species obscene and beguiling, was poetry itself. Their persistent caresses, their irregular loves (despite all mythology to the contrary), were both a spectacle and a lesson. And their consecrated nests, ever multiplying, were free to whiten the dark cypresses of Astarte.

The Phoenicians, for the sake of a prosperous voyage, placed an image of Astarte upon their ships (Venus Eu-plaea). They labored for her. Their busy trade was to carry off doves (women, girls, pretty children) for the seraglios of Asia. Their piety was, in all the establishments they created, to set up altars for Astarte, convents of abject turtledoves which fleeced all foreigners. Cyprus, Cythera were so corrupted by this cult that all the maidens of the place suffered, before marriage, this sacred pollution.

They were happy to escape at this price. For this Astaroth-Astarte, the Venus of the pirates, was not always distinguished from the other god of the Phoenicians, whom they called the King (Moloch), and who so loved children that he stole them everywhere. This King, a god of blood, fire, war, and death, took an execrable pleasure in pressing their living flesh upon his breast (of white-hot iron). If the child was not burned, he was mutilated: the iron made him into a woman.

These Molochs, these cruel merchants, masters and sultans everywhere, with their ships crammed with wretched human merchandise, with their long caravans of herds, had nothing to do with the Syrian women. Those were widows. By night, on the roofs of their houses or on the dry walls which supported a few feet of vines, they wept, dreamed, told their griefs to the moon, the equivocal Astarte. From the south and from the Dead Sea blew the sulphurous breath of the cities engulfed in sleep.

They dreamed. And never were there such powerful dreamers. Partheno-Genesis, the power of desire which even without the male is fruitful, burst forth in the form of two children the Syrian woman created by herself:

One is the woman-as-Messiah, who delivered Babylon, hitherto the slave of Nineveh; the great Semiramis, born a fish, grown into a dove, who marries all the earth, and ends by marrying her own son.

The other is a god of mourning, the Lord (Adonai or Adonis). He is born of incest, and his cult mingles tears, love, and demands that yet more incest be committed.

1864. *La bible de l'humanité,* II, 2

TERRA MATER

[In 1854, Michelet, exhausted by the Terror, which he has just described, and overwhelmed by the coup d'état, takes mud baths at Acqui, near Turin.]

Michelet in 1868
Lithograph by Lafosse

. . . On June 19, well prepared, I was finally buried, but only at half-length. In my splendid coffin of white marble, I received the first application of the black, unctuous slime, which nonetheless never dirties, being nothing more than sand. Another marble tub, beside it, receives you afterwards, and you are washed clean in an instant.

. . . On June 20, the earth invaded me higher, to the stomach, covering me almost entirely. On the 21st, I was no longer to be seen: only my face remained free to breathe. I could then discern my attendant's talent: he was a skillful sculptor in the Egyptian style. I saw myself (saving the face) completely molded in this grim garment. I could already believe myself an inhabitant of the dark kingdom.

A strange disguise! Yet nothing which need surprise us. Would I not be thus enearthed within a certain interval, in very few years, no doubt? Between this grave and the next, there is little difference. Is not our cradle, the earth, in which our race is born, also a cradle out of which to be reborn? Let us hope so. We are in good hands.

At first, I felt no more than an indiscriminate well-being. A state bordering on dreaming. After several such experiences, I could distinguish successive states, which differed among themselves.

During the first quarter of an hour, quietude. Thought, still free, examined itself. I brooded upon myself, my diseases, my origin. I accused only myself, and my ill-regulated will, the excess of that effort to relive in myself alone the life of the human race. The dead with whom I had for so long conversed attracted me, summoned me to the other shore. Nature holds me still, though longing for me there.

In the second quarter of an hour, her power increased. All ideas vanished in my profound absorption. The only notion remaining to me was *Terra mater*. I felt her very clearly, caressing and comforting, warming her wounded child. From outside? Within as well. For she penetrated me with her vivifying spirits, entered me and mingled with me, insinuating her soul in mine. Identification between us became complete. I no longer distinguished myself from her.

Until, in the last quarter of an hour, what she did not yet cover, what still remained free, my face, seemed importunate. The buried body was happy, and was myself. Not buried, my head suffered, complained: no longer being myself; at least, so I might have thought. So powerful was the marriage! and more than a marriage, between myself and the Earth! One might have said, rather, *exchange of nature.* I was the Earth, and the Earth was man. She had taken for herself my infirmity, my sin. And I, becoming Earth, had taken her life, her warmth, her youth.

Years, labors, pains, all remained in the depths of my marble coffin. I was renewed. Emerging, I had upon me a sort of unctuous phosphorescence. A certain organic element, separate from the minerals, and whose nature could not be explained, gives the effect of an animate contact, of communicating with the invisible soul, and the happy warmth which communicates it in its turn.

1868. La montagne, I, 9

KNOWN AS THE DAWN

How luminous it was, naked and fair, my desert! My very bed was set upon a rock of the great harbor of Toulon, in a humble villa, between aloes and cypresses, cactus and wild roses. Before me, that enormous sparkling basin of the sea; behind, the bare amphitheater where the world's senates might sit at their ease.

This site, so utterly African, has metallic flashes which by day are blinding. But on winter mornings, in December especially, it was filled with a divine mystery. I arose at six on the dot, when the Arsenal cannon gave the signal for work to begin. From six to seven, I experienced a splendid hour: the living (dare I say steely?) scintillation of the stars put the moon to shame, and resisted the dawn. Before it appeared, then during the battle of the two sources of light, the air's prodigious transparency permitted me to see and hear for incredible distances: I could distinguish everything for two leagues. The slightest accidents of the remote mountains, tree, rock, house, dip in the terrain—everything was revealed with the most delicate precision. I had extra senses, I seemed to possess a new being, released, winged, liberated. A limpid, austere moment, and so pure! . . . I would say to myself: "What, then—am I still a human being, still a man?"

An ineffable bluishness (which the pinkening dawn respected, dared not tinge), a sacred ether, a spirit, made all nature spirit.

Yet one felt a progress, certain deliberate and gentle transformations. A great wonder was about to come, to explode, and to eclipse all. One let it come, one was in no hurry. The imminent transfiguration, the hoped-for ravishments of light, took away nothing from the profound charm of being even now within the *divine* night, of being half hidden, without quite distinguishing oneself from the wondrous enchantment . . .

1862. *La sorcière*, Epilogue

A CHRIST OF GENTLENESS AND PATIENCE

The people, while obeying the priest, clearly distinguish him from the sacred Christ. They cultivate this ideal from age to age, they raise, they purify it in its historical reality. This Christ of gentleness and patience appears in Louis the Pious,

rejected by the bishops; in the good King Dagobert, excommunicated by the Pope; in Godefroy de Bouillon, a warrior and a Ghibelline who dies a virgin in Jerusalem, a simple *baron* of the Holy Sepulchre. The ideal grows still greater in Thomas of Canterbury, abandoned by the Church and dying for it. It attains a new degree of purity in Saint Louis, a priest-king and a king-man. Soon the generalized ideal will extend to the people; it will be realized in the fifteenth century, not only in a man of the people but in a woman as well—in Jeanne the Maid. This woman, in whom the people die on behalf of the people, will be the ultimate figure of Christ in the Middle Ages.

This transfiguration of the human race which acknowledged the image of its God in itself, which generalized what had been individual, which fixed in an eternal present what had been supposed temporary and past, which put a heaven on earth: this was the redemption of the modern world, but it seemed the death of Christianity and of Christian art. Satan uttered over the unfinished Church a huge peal of mockery; and this laughter is in the grotesques of the fif-

Michelet and Quinet resuming their lectures
at the Collège de France, in 1848
By Brouilhet

teenth and sixteenth centuries. Satan supposed he had conquered; he has never been able to learn, mad creature, that
his apparent triumph is never anything but a means. He did
not see that God is no less God for having made Himself
humanity; that the temple is not destroyed for having become as great as the world.

Meanwhile, the old world must pass, the traces of the
Middle Ages must be completely erased, we must see the
death of all that we loved, all which nourished us as children, which was our father and our mother, which sang to
us so sweetly in our cradle. In vain the old Gothic church
still raises to heaven its suppliant towers, in vain its windows
weep, in vain its saints do penance in their stone embrasures
. . . "When the rush of great waters overflows, they will
not come unto the Lord." This doomed world will vanish
with the Roman world, the Greek world, the Oriental world.
It will set its spoils alongside their spoils. God will grant it
at most, as to Hezekiah, a movement of degrees upon the
dial of Ahaz.

1833. *Histoire de France,* II, *Éclaircissements*

Michelet in 1860

HISTORY, WHICH WE SO STUPIDLY
DECLINE IN THE FEMININE

Such is History which grows, traversed "in floods" by the sap of the Just Man. But sometimes the plant stops growing, or else, on the contrary, grows too fast, monstrously. Then History, too, knows interruptions, drowsiness, sterile hibernations, or else hypertrophies, excesses or caricatures of Justice. Just like embryogeny, Micheletist history involves a veritable teratology, a class of monsters which are either an excessive, inharmonious development of certain members, or else a wasting away, an exhaustion of certain others (what Michelet calls "humiliation").

GRACE AND JUSTICE   *Among such disturbances of historical growth there occurs, in the first rank, Grace: Grace, inveterately coupled with Justice, is the (human or divine) Arbitrary—it is caprice, theocratic or tyrannical, as opposed to the regularity of Natural Law (republican law). This pair, half moral, half vitalist, produce a veritable dichotomy of History: everything in History is Grace or Justice, Fatality or Freedom, Christianity or Revolution. History is nothing but the combat of one and the other, a tragic succession of halts and advances: Syria, Alexandria, the Jews, Mariolatry, the Jesuits, the monarchy, Spinoza, Hegel, Molinos, Hobbes: all are Grace; Persia, Greece, the Vaudois, Witchcraft, the Protestants, Leibniz, Hoche, the eighteenth century: these are Justice.*

NARCOSES   *Grace, which is at the origin of all Micheletist evil, wears many masks. Consider the maleficent theme of Gambling: in the eighteenth century, politics is a gamble, a throw of the dice, Richelieu and the Capuchin Father Joseph are gamblers. Napoleon? Doomed to Chance (Buona-parte), his reign is one of farce and lottery. All of this is abominably arbitrary, monstrous moments when History seems ruled by a professor-god who has his "pets" and by his whims halts the solemn course of Justice.*

Symmetrical to the grimacing face of Italian gaming, at once farce and grandiloquence, here is another form of Grace: drowsiness, dreaming, absorption. Occasionally, History seems enchanted, fascinated, it falls asleep, loses consciousness, becomes sterile. Such sleep takes three forms: first of all, the narcotics, tobacco and alcohol; certain countries, certain periods are afflicted by them, collapse into dreams, forget the duty to engender, think of nothing but smoking and drinking, and abandon History, vanish from its fruitful surface—Turkey, for example.

Next, the Novel: the novel is an absorbing power, it deflects from History, i.e., from Justice; it is par excellence the order of the Arbitrary, of Grace, of Illusion: the Spain of Cervantes and of Loyola is infatuated with the novel, with the phantasmagoria of miracle, and thereby it loses the thread of History, it disappears from movement.

Last, Boredom: certain centuries, certain countries are bored, a sign that History stops growing: the Middle Ages yawn, held in a state midway between sleep and waking; the dawning nineteenth century, under Napoleon's tyranny, is bored to death; it produces only dead works such as that of the "barbaro-Breton" Chateaubriand, or Adolphe, *the novel of boredom, or Mme de Staël's pale and diffuse* Corinne.

COPYIST AND HONNÊTE-HOMME   *These halts of History produce two types of humanity equally execrated by Mi-*

chelet: the copyist and the honnête-homme. *A sleeping History produces worse than nothingness: senility. The Middle Ages rapidly becomes a civilization of copyists: in 1300, architecture merely repeats itself to infinity: no more songs, no more books. The churches steal from each other; Aix-la-Chapelle is made from the marbles of Ravenna; an entire society remains captive to the first and last word of the Middle Ages: Imitation.*

The same humiliation occurs in the monarchic centuries; here the medieval copyist has become l'honnête-homme, *a sterile figure, cushioned and sickly like Montaigne, weak and negative like the petty lord formed by the classical educators, Molière, Fénelon, Rousseau. Contrasting with which—like Justice with Grace—are the hero and the citizen.*

THE WORLD-AS-WOMAN *Evidently these themes, organic in intention, since they all define a halt of historical growth, are also themes of humor: Grace, Gambling, Tobacco, Alcohol, the Novel, Boredom—so many figures of the Sterile and the Lax, of that dry Death which occasionally threatens the ideal unctuosity of a History fecundated by the Just Man.*

Now, the constitutive character of Justice is its power of solidification. The responsibility of Justice is to draw in the infinity of historical substance the lineaments of the future City. The beginnings of History are therefore occupied—unless we consider certain peoples-of-the-light such as Persia or Greece—by an ambiguous Night ready to receive the seed of Justice. This milieu of darkness is the World-as-Woman.

The World-as-Woman is those countries, those peoples and ages deprived of the male principle of Justice, and doomed thereby to a sort of dry or licentious widowhood, in any case a sterile one. This explains the ambiguous character of the World-as-Woman: sometimes it is softness and excess, scabrous languor as in the case of primitive Syria, of the Dionysiac religions, of Molinism, and of Quietism; sometimes it is aridity, grim and gar-

rulous harshness, the dryness of the pebble and the razor, as in the case of the peoples of the Book (Jews and Mohammedans). The common characteristic is sterility, or at the very least the disorganized and inhuman germination of the parthenogenetic world.

SATAN AND THE WITCH   *The sexualized opposition of female Grace and virile Justice actually organizes all of Micheletist history, for the Just Man here assumes figures as numerous as those of Grace. The first form of Justice: Satan, "bizarre name of a still-young freedom, at first militant, negative, later creative, increasingly fruitful," and his hypostasis, the Witch.*

   The Witch is, in the Middle Ages, the instrument of medicine, which is for Michelet a technique of penetration. Moreover, she possesses all the characteristics of a male principle: she is an essence (like the homunculus of the spermists) and she is an aperient action. Her feminine name must not lead us astray (is not Histoire, *too, wrongly feminine?): more than a woman, she is a matron, i.e., a superlative and complete sex, uniting male power and female power. (We shall see later that for Michelet this ultra-sex is of feminine dominance.) The Witch, moreover, can in those moments when history halts altogether (at the end of the Middle Ages, for example) experience a kind of sterile degeneration; she becomes a professional, i.e., the beneficent theme of fruitfulness is here interrupted by the maleficent theme of imitation, of the mechanical.*

THE HERO   *Another capital form of the Just Man: the hero. The Micheletist hero, the man who deposits Justice within History (Luther, Rabelais, Kosciuszko, Hoche, Leibniz, the eighteenth century), is also a complete, i.e., ambiguous male; he possesses a superhuman force of conduction, and moreover pos-*

sesses a weapon that is precisely epic: Laughter. Laughter is a male power, it destroys, explodes, and fertilizes. For example, it is Luther's joy which shakes up and germinates the sterile Church, and it is Desmoulins's laughter which terrifies and checkmates Robespierre-as-Cat-and-Priest, as elsewhere the Sign of the Cross disorganizes and overcomes the Devil.

Michelet himself becomes a hero, i.e., doubly sexed, genitor of Justice at the heart of female Grace. But this was an intermittent power in him, which he possessed only at certain paroxystic moments, and following certain initiations. This is what Michelet calls heroization. Heroization is the power of seeing and resuscitating Justice in History, which is properly the function of the Magus: having by certain readings reached a higher zone of knowledge, Michelet makes himself the conductor of the Just Man, bridegroom and father of History. This power of heroization, moreover, is transmitted in the manner of a seed, it can come only from other heroes. Michelet has thus been initiated, heroized by Virgil, Vico, and Beethoven.

LEGISTS Naturally, there are caricatures of the Just Man, there are historical types which borrow from the Just Man his principal rigor but remain sterile nonetheless. For example, there is the Law. The legists—a great Micheletist theme, common moreover to Saint-Simon and to Comte—take various forms: we recognize them under various names at many moments of History. Their role is in truth an ambiguous one: it seems that in the Middle Ages, and insofar as he stood against the Ghibelline shapelessness,* the Guelf legist had a creative function. But once the sixteenth century produces heroes, i.e., superlative men, doubly sexed, the legists are no longer anything but a futile and

---

*The Guelf–Ghibelline pair is a Micheletist theme. The Ghibelline is the German, i.e., the devotion of man to man, Grace, the World-as-Woman. The Guelf (of Roman ancestry) is reason, is Law.

maleficent sect, unremittingly cast into the discredit attached to the Mechanical and the Scholastic.

The Jacobins, the great priest-society, are also demonetized by their legistical character; they are makers of a Law which is merely the caricature of the Just Man, since it lacks the essential, i.e., the incubating virtue of the ambisexed People. History itself is a value only if legal history, a paper-history, is transcended by a cordial history, a tradition-history.

PENETRATION   *But the two major figures of Grace and Justice are Christianity and the Revolution. The first is milieu, the second a force: which is to say that they are eternal, and their rivalry is on the order of a polarity. This is posited by the great preface to the* Histoire de la Révolution: *on the stage of History, there is never anything but "two great phenomena, two principles, two actors and two persons, Christianity and the Revolution." This milieu and this force are complementary, like the sexes: they are two angles, one salient, one reentering.* History is an amorous combat.*

The very action by which the Just Man fecundates History is presented as a penetration. That this virtually erotic movement borrows its name from ethics and is called Action† *must not mislead us. The greatest of the Micheletist heroes, the eighteenth century, is called Action; by which is meant* act *in the genetic sense of the term. Nor should the moralizing phrases on education deceive us: education, having become a purely rhetorical theme among Michelet's radical-socialist epigones, is actually, in the original system, an aperient technique, a technique of deposit and germination. Michelet himself as educator (he has been em-*

---

*"Christianity and the Revolution are like salient and reentering angles, symmetrically opposed, if not mutually hostile." —Michelet to Victor Hugo, May 4, 1956
†The theme of action is to be found in August Cieskowski (1838), in Bakunin, and in Marx around 1843–45.

balmed long enough in this pious legend!) is an opener and a discoverer. His knowledge is a rape, a violation. Did he not want, moreover, to take as his motto this inscription from an old medieval epic: Penetrabit *(it will penetrate)?*

THEOPHANY OF THE REVOLUTION   *The fertilization of Grace by Justice is crowned by a mystic birth which justifies all previous History, summarizes it and brings it to an end: the Revolution of '89. The amorous combat prepares the City, History dies in giving birth to it. Caused by all that has preceded it, the Revolution is nonetheless not a goal, in the evolutionist sense of the word: as the essence of Justice, it has always existed, and has merely flowed like a more or less thwarted germinal fluid.*

There are, one might say, two Revolutions: an (eternal) Revolution-principle and a Revolution-incarnate (that of '89). So that, paradoxically, it is the historical Revolution which retroactively reveals its infinite prologue: it is the sovereign drama which explains all anterior History. It explodes like the incarnatus est *of Justice, it interrupts time in order to summarize and consummate it. Itself, moreover, does not participate in time: in it, there is no duration: a minute here is a century, or rather: "neither century, nor year, nor month, nor day, nor hour . . . Time no longer existed, time had perished."* *

Thereby, the insertion of the Revolution into History, its "historicity," is not at all the fruit of a maturation, and for Michelet there is no determinism which has impelled the monarchy to succumb in 1792 rather than earlier or later. Ideally, the Revolution, being an essence, has its place everywhere, it is logical and necessary at any point in the ages. Michelet has himself

---

*Jaurès: "In those hours so full, so wonderfully concentrated, when minutes were worth centuries, death alone answers to the impatience of minds and to the haste of affairs."

assumed this ubiquity of the Revolution by deciding to narrate it, to celebrate it (as one celebrates the sacrifice of the Mass) when it suits him, and not according to an altogether temporal logic of History. We know that having arrived in his History of France at Louis XI, and preparing with a certain tedium to begin on Modern Times, Michelet happened to read inside the bell tower of Rheims the revolutionary principle, the claims of the poor inscribed in the circle of the people around the monarchy. It is here that he realized that the Revolution was a totality which nourished every moment of History and that it could consequently be posited at any point in time without thereby troubling the profound order of events: it was always in its place, wherever it was. Michelet had no scruple about writing his Revolution between his Middle Ages and his Renaissance.

CHRISTOMORPHISM OF THE REVOLUTION *But just as any amorous combat is only a postponed identity, so the Revolution is only the usurping figure of Christianity.* "This God had to have his second epoch, had to appear on earth in his incarnation of '89." The Revolution is constructed like the Christian incarnation. Not only, as we have just seen, does it interrupt, sum up, and fulfill time, but it also possesses its Last Supper (the Federations of '90), its blood and tears ("These laws, this blood, and these tears it gave to all, saying: This is my blood, drink"), even its Passion ("In the eyes of Europe, let it be known, France will always have but one inexpiable name, which is her true name in eternity: the Revolution"). And she has not even failed to know the threat of a historical disaggregation; the revolutionary sects broke up the Revolution, just as the Jansenists, the Molinists, and the rest exhausted Christianity.*

The Revolution also has its pope, who is Michelet. Michelet

*It will be recalled that the theme of a "transformed" Christianity (the eternal Gospel) is central in Michelet.

is the total priest, he receives in his own body the god's sufferings and humiliations. Michelet is the one who discovers the pangs of the Revolution, takes them on himself, dies of them, and finally redeems them because he explains them. To be a historian is ultimately to approach the Revolution in ceremonial terms, and the entire Micheletist narrative is processional—Michelet ascends to the altar of the sacrifice: "I bore all this past, as I would have borne the ashes of my father or of my son."

Michelet's anticlericalism is therefore no more than a transference, and of the most naïve kind. All the characteristics of priesthood are stripped from the confessional priest and entrusted to the lay priest: "The Church is concerned with the world, it teaches us our business; well and good. We shall teach it God." Biography can have its part in this movement: at the bedside of his dying friend Madame Dumesnil, Michelet had seen himself supplanted by a priest. Cause or sign? His lay priesthood corresponded quite closely to the protest of a robbed man, who lays claim to his goods and reconstitutes them. The truth is that, in Michelet's eyes, the lay pontificate constitutes a delicious rape of consciences: the Revolution-as-god authorizes its priest to perform infinite acts of opening and expansion.

THE SUSPENSION OF HISTORY   Only this priesthood is like the other; and it makes celibacy similarly mandatory—at least a spiritual celibacy: if he wants to espouse the Revolution, Michelet must strip himself of his own history.* Since the Revolution fulfills time, what can be the time that comes after the Revolution and that is precisely the time in which Michelet is living? Nothing, if not a post-History. The nineteenth century is quite awkward; why does it continue, since it has no further place in the combat of freedom? And yet it exists. Then what is

* At the moment of writing his *Histoire de la Révolution*, Michelet purifies himself: he renounces a "degrading" liaison with an old friend of his wife's.

it? Nothing but a suspension, a time of grace or condemnation, but in any case a supernumerary time, like the Time of the Patience of God, bestowed upon Christians between the death of Christ and the Last Judgment. The Revolution being the glorious advent of the Just Man (i.e., the Kingdom of God), everything which separates the Revolution from the future City is an incomprehensible time—in other words, a time reprieved from History no longer participating in its signification.

Michelet lived in this suspension of History with the same astonishment as a Christian in the reign of Otho or of Galba. His political struggles must not deceive us: as a matter of fact, Michelet in no way participated in the work of his age: his numerous evasions and escapes are always essential; his instances of courage are accessory, decorative (which must not make their sincerity suspect). Deaf to his time, a Republican only in History,* troubled, bitter in the presence of that History which persisted in surviving its own fulfillment, he could make the nineteenth century enter into that trial of time only as an Apocalypse. This is the meaning of his last, extremely nihilistic preface, and of the (unjustified) interest he took in Grainville's† poem "The Last Man" (which he quotes as an appendix to his last work): a beloved theme—sweetness of tears, grandeur of refusal, "triumphant loss in emulation of victory" ‡—that solitude of the Last Man of a bygone but fulfilled world.

* The pertinent expression of Madame Quinet.
† Died in 1805.
‡ Montaigne's phrase.

Henceforth, men increasingly resorted to seeking the brutal illusion of drink, of dreams in fumigation. Two new demons were born: alcohol and tobacco.

Arabic alcohol, *eau-de-vie* distilled in the West in the thirteenth century and still, in the sixteenth, a very expensive remedy for the sick, will be diffused, offering all the temptations of false energy, barbaric overstimulation, a brief moment of frenzy, the flame followed by the moral chill of the void, by humiliation.

And also, narcotics; nicotia (now known as tobacco) substitutes an indifferent reverie for serious thought, causes all ills to be forgotten, and their remedies as well. It makes life undulate, like the faint smoke whose spiral rises and fades away at its own sweet will. Vain vapor in which man is dissolved, unconcerned with himself, with others, with any true affection.

Two enemies of love, two demons of solitude, antipathetic to social concerns, deadly to generation. The man who smokes has no need for women; a widower even in marriage; his love is this fume into which the best of himself passes and vanishes.

This fatal isolation begins precisely with the seventeenth century, upon the appearance of tobacco. Our sailors of Bayonne and Saint-Jean-de-Luz, who brought it in so cheaply, began smoking to excess, three and four times a day. Their natural indifference was thereby strangely increased. They kept apart from women, and the latter even more explicitly turned away from them. From the inception of this drug, we can foresee its effect. It has suppressed the kiss.

The lovely women of Bayonne, proud, bold, and cynical, declared to Judge Lancre that this base custom of their men caused them to abandon their families and to participate in the witches' Sabbath as sailors' wives: "Better the Devil's ass than our husbands' mouths."

This in 1610. A fatal date which opens the roads on which men and women follow divergent paths.

If the wife is solitary, stripped of her husband's support, I fear she must take a lover, who will be this fierce consoler, this husband of fire and ice, the demon of spirituous liqueurs. It is this demon who will increasingly become the true King of the Sabbath.

It will not be long before the witches' Sabbath itself becomes useless. The witch, in her attic, alone with the liquid devil which burns and disturbs her, will indulge in her wild orgy, creating for herself all the shames of the Sabbath.

Women throughout the north have yielded to alcohol. And men everywhere to tobacco. Two deserts and two solitudes. Whole nations, whole races have already collapsed, lost in this mute abyss, whose depths are indifference to the pleasures of generation and the annihilation of love.

In vain have the women of our own day and age mournfully submitted in order to regain their men. They have suffered tobacco and endured the smoker, who is antipathetic to them. Cowardly and futile weakness. Do they not see that this man, so utterly content with his insipid pleasure, cannot, will not turn to them? The Turk has closed his harem. Let him, in the same way, depart by the path which our Oriental predecessors have followed into death.

1857. Histoire de France, XI, 17

HISTORY STOPS: THE NOVEL

One thing disturbs at this moment, and appears entirely new, of infinite consequence—*the Novel.*

The history of the Jews, at whatever level of seriousness, transpired against a fictive background—the arbitrary miracle, in which it pleased God to choose among the lowest, indeed among the unworthiest, a *Saviour,* a liberator, an avenger of the people. In the Captivity or in court intrigues, sudden fortunes cast imaginations on the path of the unexpected. The splendid historical novels of Joseph, Ruth, Tobit, Esther, Daniel, and many more appeared. Always based on two givens: *the good exile,* who, by the interpretation of dreams and financial cunning, becomes minister or favorite—or else *the woman beloved of God,* who makes a great marriage, attains to glory, seduces the enemy, and (astonishingly enough, in contrast with the Mosaic notions) is the *Saviour of the people.* For Moses she was impure, dangerous, had brought about the Fall. But it is precisely the unexpected choice which the novel seizes upon.* God makes the woman a snare, utilizes her seduction, and through her brings about the Fall of the man he has doomed.

Love is a lottery, Grace is a lottery. There is the essence of the novel. It is the contrary of history, not only because it

---

*"Monsieur, what is the novel? Madame, it is what is in your mind at this moment. For since you are concerned neither with your country nor with knowledge nor even with religion, you are brewing what Sterne calls a hobbyhorse and what I am calling a pretty little *doll.*" —We have an insipid novel. Why? Because we have no great poetry. —Michelet's note

subordinates great collective interests to an individual destiny but because it does not favor the ways of that difficult preparation which in history produces events. It prefers to show us the lucky casts of the dice which chance occasionally produces, to flatter us with the idea that the impossible frequently becomes possible. By this hope, this pleasure, this interest, it wins its reader, spoiled from the start, who follows it avidly, to the point where he will forgo talent, even skill. The chimerical mind is interested in the story, in the *affair*—wants it to *turn out well*.

1864. *La bible de l'humanité,* II, 6

HISTORY STOPS: BOREDOM

[*The fifteenth century*] . . . And what was left of so much laughter? Nothing but the aggravation of evils, discouragement, despair of any good, boredom and heartsickness. It appears that the light has failed; the weather is not black but gray. A monotonous cloud discolors creation. And when the indefatigable clock rings out the usual hours, one yawns; when a singsong voice murmurs on in the old Latin, one yawns. Everything is foreseen; one hopes for nothing in this world. Things will always turn out to be the same. The unquestionable boredom of tomorrow makes one yawn today, and the prospect of the days and years of boredom to come oppresses the future, disgusts one with living. From brain to belly, from belly to mouth, the automatic and doomed convulsion goes on distending the jaws with neither end nor remedy. A true malady which pious Brittany acknowledges, though setting it down to the Devil's wiles. He crouches out there in the woods, say the Breton peasants; to the man who passes by herding his cattle, he sings out Vespers and all the canonical hours, and makes him yawn his way to death.

1855. *Histoire de France,* VII, *La Renaissance,*
Introduction

Only one original feature was left for Bonaparte's age, one new genre: *the literature of boredom.*

Which astonished Napoleon. He sometimes read the new books, and found nothing in them. He consulted Fiévée, whom he kept on the premises. Once he ordered one of his ministers to write a History of France. And obtained nothing. Vacancy, nothingness, that new king of the world, nothingness alone answered him.

The noisy, garrulous salons of the Directory, now carefully spied on by the listeners Fouché sent into them, though they dared not close, had gradually lost their members and emptied out. Which sounded the signal for a universal yawn. Once the Tribunate was closed, its extremely brilliant speaker Benjamin Constant wrote his novel *Adolphe* (1802), in which we see that love, the period's sole resource, is no defense against boredom. Madame de Staël, on her side, produced the extremely diffuse novel *Delphine* (1802), and then in *Corinne* the insipid character of Oswald, an indecision which turns to spleen.

Finally, a very great writer, Sénancour, does not even try to be bored *à deux.* In his *Obermann,* he seeks life in solitude, in nature (not a painted, whimsical nature, like the false nature of *Atala*), but in the true, sublime nature of the Alps.

Even here, in his Valais asylum, boredom is loyal to him, and he finds it wherever he turns. It has taken possession of his entire being.

Boredom is so much the master of the age that Chateaubriand, who of late had taken it upon himself to comfort us by the lure of his old memories, himself admits that his religion, evoked in the *Génie du Christianisme,* has neither calmed nor consoled him. Whence *René,* that admission of despairing melancholy. —Singular episode which one is amazed to find amid this Christian encyclopedia.

Finally, after so much talk, so many sighs and false appeals to death, death comes and says: Here I am!

Grainville writes, kills himself. Here is something frank and decisive—which must silence all the chatterers.

Le Dernier homme, much superior in conception to any modern work, but pallid in execution, reveals thereby a profound feature of truth, being visibly conceived in despair (1798–1804).

1872. *Histoire du XIXe siècle,* III, *Waterloo,* I, 9.

DRY DEATH: PEOPLES OF THE BOOK

The three *peoples of the Book,* the Jew and his two sons, the Christian and the Moslem, cultivating the Word and neglecting life, rich in words, poor in works, have forgotten the Earth. *Terra mater.* Blasphemers . . . Consider the nakedness of the old Graeco-Byzantine world. Consider the sullen deserts of Castile, so harsh and barren. Consider all the canals of India abandoned by the British. Persia, that paradise of God, what is Persia? A Moslem cemetery. From Judea to Tunis to Morocco, and indeed from Athens to Genoa, all those bald peaks which stare down at the Mediterranean have lost their crowns of growth, of forests. And will they return? Never. If the ancient gods, the strong and active races under whom these shores flourished, were to emerge from their tombs today, they would say: "Sad *peoples of the Book,* of grammar and of words, of futile subtleties, what have you made of Nature?"

1864. *Bible de l'humanité,* II, 9

A FIGURE OF JUSTICE: THE WITCH

The great and powerful doctor of the Renaissance, Paracelsus, in burning the learned books of all ancient medicine, those of the Latins, the Jews, and the Arabs, declares he has learned nothing save from the people's medicine, *from old wives, from shepherds, and from executioners:* the latter often being skillful surgeons (setters of broken and disjointed bones) and good veterinarians.

I have no doubt that his admirable and inspired book on the *Diseases of Women,* the first ever written on this great subject, so profound and so touching, derived chiefly from the experience of the women themselves, those from whom the others sought assistance: I mean the witches who, everywhere, were midwives. Never in those days would a woman have admitted a male physician, have confided in him, have told him her secrets. The witches were the only onlookers and were, for women especially, the sole physicians.

What we know best of their medicine is that they used most frequently, for the most diverse needs, both to calm and to stimulate, a large family of plants—ambiguous and highly dangerous—which rendered the greatest services. These are (rightly) called the Consolers *(Solanaceae).*

A huge and popular family, most of whose species are abundant, ever underfoot, in the hedges, everywhere. A family so numerous that a single genus has some eight hundred species. Nothing easier to find, nothing more common. But these plants are mostly of very dubious use: it required boldness to specify the doses, perhaps the boldness of genius.

Let us start from the bottom of the scale in discussing their energies. The first are simply potherbs and good to eat (eggplants, tomatoes, misnamed love apples). Others of these innocent species are peace and gentleness themselves, the mulleins (common mullein or Aaron's rod), so useful for fomentations.

Next above these, we find a plant already suspect, which many believed to be a poison, a plant sweet initially, then bitter, which seems to say with Jonathan: "I did but taste a little honey, and lo I must die." But this death is useful, it is the absorption of pain. Bittersweet, as it is called, must be the first attempt of a bold homeopathy, which gradually ascended to the most dangerous poisons. The slight irritation, the prickling which it causes could designate it for the remedy of the most prevalent diseases of these times, those of the skin.

The pretty girl in despair at finding herself covered with hateful rashes, pimples, open sores, came weeping for help. In women, the afflictions were even worse. The breast, the most delicate object in nature, and its vessels, which under the skin form an incomparable blossom, is, by its readiness to become suffused, engorged, the most perfect instrument of pain. Harsh, pitiless, ceaseless pain. How readily she would have accepted any poison! She did not bargain with the witch but thrust into her hands the poor, throbbing breast.

From bittersweet, far too weak, one ascended to black morels, which have a somewhat stronger action. This calmed the pain for several days. Then the woman returned in tears: "Well, tonight you come back . . . I'll find you something. You need it: it is a great poison."

The witch was risking a great deal. In those days, no one realized that, when applied externally or taken in very small doses, poisons were remedies. The plants which were grouped together under the name "witchgrass" seemed ministers of death. Found in her hands, they would have accused her of being a poisoner or a maker of evil spells. A blind mob, cruel in proportion to its fear, could, some morning, stone her to death, or force her to undergo the proof by water (noyade). Or else, still more terrible, they could drag her by a rope round her neck into the churchyard, where she would have been made into a pious celebration, edifying the people by being burned at the stake.

Yet she runs the risk, goes looking for the terrible plants; she does so in the evenings, or at dawn, when there is less risk of being found out. Yet a little shepherd boy was there and says to the village: "You should have seen her, creeping through the ruins of some abandoned hut, peering this way and that, murmuring something . . . ! Oh, she scared me, all right . . . If she had found me, I was lost . . . She could have changed me into a lizard, or a toad, or a bat . . . She picked a nasty weed, the nastiest I've ever seen—a sickly, pale yellow one with red and black marks on it, like the flames of hell. Worst of all, the whole stem was hairy as a man, with long sticky black hairs. And she yanked it up with a sigh, and all of a sudden I lost sight of her. She couldn't have run so fast; she must have flown away . . . That woman is a terror! What a danger for us, for the whole countryside!"

Certainly the plant is alarming: it is henbane, a cruel and dangerous poison, but a powerful emollient, a gentle sedative cataplasm which soothes, calms, lulls pain, often cures it altogether.

Another of these poisons, *belladonna,* so named no doubt in gratitude, was effective in calming the convulsions which sometimes occur in childbirth, which add danger to danger, terror to the terror of this supreme moment. But a motherly hand insinuated this gentle poison, lulled the mother to sleep, and charmed the sacred portal; the child, just as today, when chloroform is used, achieved its own freedom, and flung itself into life.

1862. *La sorcière,* I, 9

THE REVOLUTION BELONGS EVERYWHERE

I entered with Louis XI upon the monarchic centuries. I was about to commit myself to them when a sort of accident inspired me with second thoughts. One day, passing through Rheims, I examined in great detail the magnificent cathedral, the splendid church of the Rites of Coronation.

The inner cornice along which one can circumambulate the church eighty feet above the floor, revealed it to be enchanting—a flowering wealth, a permanent paean. In the empty immensity, one thinks one still hears the great official clamor, what used to be called *the voice of the people.* One imagines one sees at the windows the birds released when the clergy, anointing the king, made the pact between throne and church. Coming back outside, under the porch, to the enormous view which embraces all of Champagne, I had reached the last little steeple, just above the choir. Here, a strange spectacle amazed me: the round tower was embellished with a garland of executed criminals. One had a rope around his neck, another had lost an ear. The mutilated were even more melancholy than the dead. How right they were! What a hideous contrast! So—the church of festivities, the bride, had put on this lugubrious ornament for a wedding necklace! This pillory of the people was placed above the altar! But their tears, could they not have fallen from the vaults upon the heads of kings? Dreadful unction of the Revolution, of the wrath of God. "I shall not understand the monarchic centuries if first of all, before everything else, I do not establish within myself the soul and the faith of the people"—so I determined, and after Louis XI, I wrote the *Revolution* (1845–53).

1869. *Histoire de France,* I, Preface

CHRISTOMORPHISM OF THE REVOLUTION

You who weep, come to this God, for He weeps.
You who suffer, come to Him, for He cures.
You who tremble, come to Him, for he smiles.
You who pass, come to Him, for he abides.
—Victor Hugo. *Les contemplations,* III

Michelet's son-in-law, Alfred Dumesnil: "my other self"

Paris, May 4 [1856]

As we move on in life, our affections are concentrated, and every day I feel more distinctly how much you mean to me—how much I belong to you.

All of France has echoed to your great heart. By which we are delighted, not surprised.

But your people—and I am of that number—think of you, and beneath that glow of glory and of immortality, we think of your present state. This new volume disconcerts us. It is a terrible thing to exhume one's past in this fashion . . . The world, dear monsieur, the world that you sustain with your work, begs you to turn your thoughts to it. I believe it would beg you as well to sacrifice a few lines—the six verses on the Crucifix.

We are beaten about the head with that crucifix, for us it has become the Indian tomahawk. Myself, I shall die in the faith I put in print in 1847, in the first volume of my *Revolution*. Christianity and the Revolution are like salient and reentering angles, symmetrically opposed, if not hostile. When Christianity is no longer in a vampiric state (neither dead nor alive), but an honest corpse, at peace and in its grave, as are India, Egypt, and Rome, then, and then only, shall we defend all that is defensible within it. Until then, no. It is the enemy.

Your authority is so great, a word from you weighs so much in the balance of things, that each of us watches closely the point to which you incline. And indeed, apart from this one page, this memory of the dead past, your book, full of such great passions, seems inspired in every line by the living faith of nature.

I take your hand in brotherhood, and thank you with all my heart. A thousand tender wishes for your family.

J. Michelet

—Quoted in J.-M. Carré, *Michelet et son temps*

THE FRENCH CRIME

Frenchmen of every circumstance, of every class and of every party, remember one thing, you have on this earth only one true friend, and that friend is France. You will always be guilty, in the eyes of the eternal coalition of aristocracies, of one crime, of having, fifty years ago, sought to deliver the world. They have not forgiven it, they will not forgive it. You are always their peril. You may be distinguished among yourselves by different party names, but you are, as Frenchmen, condemned together. In the eyes of Europe, let it be known, France will always have but one inexpiable name, which is her true name in eternity: the Revolution.

1846. *Le peuple,* Preface

THE APOCALYPSE OF OUR TIME

One of today's most serious, and least remarked phenomena, is that the gait of time has entirely altered. It has doubled its steps in a strange fashion. In a single lifetime (of ordinary length, seventy-two years), I have seen two great revolutions which once might have taken place at intervals of two thousand years.

I was born during the great territorial revolution, and I shall have seen the dawn of the great industrial revolution.

Born under the Terror of Babeuf, I see, before I die, the Terror of the Internationale.

Several times the same panic has created in my lifetime what was believed to be a remedy: military government, the Caesar of Austerlitz, the Caesar of Sedan.

A great change which, seizing public attention, has distracted it from a phenomenon no less grave and no less general: the creation of the greatest empire ever seen beneath the sun, the British Empire, ten times more far-flung than those of Bonaparte and of Alexander the Great.

Never has death scored such triumphs round the globe. For if Napoleon in only ten years (1804–14), according to his own figures, killed seventeen hundred thousand Frenchmen, and no doubt as many Germans, Russians, etc., England, in a famous trial, accused one of her governors of having killed by famine, in one year, *millions* of Indians. By this mere fact, one may judge what a hundred years of colonial tyranny can be, imposed without control in an unknown world upon a population of two hundred million souls.

But if the destructive forces have scored such triumphs, the creative forces are no less astounding by their miracles. And this so recently! I seem to be dreaming when I think that these incredible things have occurred in one man's lifetime. I was born in '98. This was the period when M. Watt, having long since made his discovery, put it to work in manufacture (Watt and Bolton), producing without measure his workmen of copper and iron, by which England would soon have the power of four hundred million men. This prodigious English world, born with me, has declined. And this terrible century, applying to warfare its mechanical genius, yesterday produced the victory of Prussia.

Those who believe that the past contains the future, and that history is a stream forever flowing one and the same, forever impelling the same waters between its banks, must here reflect and see that very often a century is opposed to the preceding century, sometimes furnishing it a harsh denial. As much as the eighteenth century, upon the death of Louis XIV, advanced lightly on the wing of ideas and of individual activity, by just so much our own century with its great machines (the factory and the barracks), blindly harnessing the masses, has advanced into fatality.

Consider that to these great phenomena here below there corresponds up above, very faithfully, a little bell: it is philosophy, which says the very same things. To the fatalism of 1815 and of Hegel succeeds the medical, physiological fatalism of Virchow, Robin, and Littré.

In general, this materialist history might be expressed in three words: *Socialism, Militarism,* and *Industrialism.* Three things which engender and destroy each other.

Babeuf's Terror produced Bonaparte as well as his victories, which is to say that a dawning Socialism, by the panic it caused, produced the triumph of Militarism.

And Militarism, what did it encounter in its great struggle? Invariably, the English gold created by the industrial power which paid and armed Europe. A power vanquished at Austerlitz, victorious at Waterloo.

1872. *Histoire du XIXe siècle,* I, *Origine des Bonaparte,*
Preface

SUBSIDENCE INTO SLEEP UNDERGROUND *Piranesi*
"Vast underground prisons, filled with tortures and trophies, infernal labyrinths where one can wander eternally without ever finding one's way, endless staircases which offer some hope of climbing out into daylight, which one climbs and climbs in vain, without being able to reach anything but the exhaustion of despair." —*La Révolution,* V, 2

DEATH-AS-SLEEP AND
DEATH-AS-SUN

In this vast amorous combat between Justice and Grace, the historian-as-priest cannot remain impartial. Objective, i.e., obedient to the object of history, yes, and Michelet has always claimed to be so. He could not endure being called a poet more than a historian. But where is the real stake of historical labor? Is it to rediscover a Pointillist order of details, as Taine and the scientific school would have it? or else the plenitude, the vast unctuosity of the past? For Michelet the historical mass is not a puzzle to reconstitute, it is a body to embrace. The historian exists only to recognize a warmth.

THE DOCUMENT AS VOICE   *The roots of historical truth are therefore the documents as voices, not as witnesses. Michelet considers in them, exclusively, that quality of having been an attribute of life, the privileged object to which clings a kind of residual memory of past bodies. Thus, the closer the document comes to a voice, the less it departs from the warmth which has produced it, and the more it is the true foundation of historical credibility. This is why the oral document is ultimately superior to the written document, the Legend to the texts. The national tradition is the historian's best source; it is, in the dominant facts, "very grave, very certain, of an authority superior to all* the others." The voice of the people affords Michelet a warmer memory that is more "linked together" than all the writings of legislators and witnesses. Why? It is because collective consciousness is a better conductor than the "dry" consciousness (dry = disjointed, heterogeneous) of individuals (unless they themselves are the People, Heroes, i.e., plenitude, a warm, moist, and ultimately incubating milieu).

MICHELET-AS-OEDIPUS   *The historian is not at all a "reader" of the past, and if he reorganizes History, it is not on the level of ideas, of forces, of causes or systems, but on the level of each carnal death. The historian's duties are not established in terms of the general concept of historical truth, but only confronting each dead man of history; his function is not of an intellectual order, it is at once of a social and a sacred order. The historian is in fact a civil magistrate in charge of administering the estate of the dead (a formula Michelet derives from Camoëns in the Indies). This civil magistracy is doubled of course by a priesthood: it is less a matter of keeping vigil over the memory of the dead than of completing by a magical action what in their lives may have been absurd or mutilated. The historian is an Oedipus (he retrospectively solves human enigmas). History's dead never understand why they have lived, for, according to the Sophoclean formula, life is intelligible only when death has provided it with an irremissible goal. The historian is precisely the magus who receives from the dead their actions, their sufferings, their sacrifices, and gives them a place in History's universal memory.*

TRUTH OF ASSASSINATED MEN   *Caesar under Brutus's knife, Becket under that of Reginald Fitzurse, the Duke of Orléans under those of the Burgundians, the Duke de Guise under that of Henri III—each of these has been himself, achieved his true stature, only once he was dead, lying at his assassin's feet like a new man, mysterious, unaccustomed, different from the old one by all the distance of a revelation, that revelation produced by the ultimate coherence of a destiny. This new man is the historical man. If these prone and still-warm dead men are saved from nothingness, it is because Michelet was already gazing upon them, the historian was already taking them over, already explaining their lives to them. He was drawing from them a raw, blind, chaotic, incomplete, absurd life, and restoring to them a clear life, a full life, embellished by an ultimate historical signification, linked to the great living (i.e., genetic) surface of History.*

Thus, the historian is the man who has reversed Time, who turns back to the place of the dead and recommences their life in a clear and useful direction; he is the demiurge who links what was scattered, discontinuous, incomprehensible: he weaves together the threads of all lives, he knits up the great fraternity of the dead, whose formidable displacement, through Time, forms that extension of History which the historian leads while walking backwards, gathered within his gaze which decides and discloses.

TO LIVE OUT DEATH *The historian, funereal magistrate, must therefore approach death more closely than others. He must live out death, i.e., he must love it; it is at this price alone that, having entered into a sort of primitive communion with the dead, he can exchange with them the signs of life. This ceremonial of the approach to death is Michelet's entire history.*

And this approach is an exorcism. Death becomes the necessary and sufficient object of the historian's life. Michelet devours the dead ("I have drunk the black blood of the dead"); he is therefore one of them. Under the moral finality of Micheletist

History, there is an intimate finality which designates the entire past as Michelet's nourishment. All of History discloses itself so that Michelet may live on it. A magical relationship consecrates the world as the historian's nutriment, marks it out as the goal of a consummation. "The gods," Homer had already said, "determine human fates and decide the fall of men, in order that future generations can compose their songs." At the heart of every resurrectional myth (and we know only too well this ambition of Micheletist History*), there is a ritual of assimilation. The resurrection of the past is not a metaphor; it is actually a kind of sacred manducation, a domestication of Death. The life Michelet restores to the dead is assigned a funereal coefficient so heavy that resurrection becomes the original essence, absolutely fresh and virgin of death, as in those dreams where one sees a dead person living, while knowing perfectly well that the person is dead.

In the Micheletist resurrection of the past, death is heavy. It is neither paradise nor grave, it is the very existence of the dead person, but dreamed, reconciling in itself the familiar (touching) features of life and the solemn knowledge of death. In this fashion, every flaw is corrected, every misstep conquered between life and death, between the timorous solitude of the living historian and the communion of all the dead who are no longer afraid. It is for this that Michelet so readily shifted his own organism to the countless people of the dead; constantly touching death, like Antaeus his mother earth, he attached himself to History as to the apprenticeship of his own death.

DEATH-AS-SLEEP *Unfortunately, not all deaths possess that revealing virtue which discloses the style of an existence. Some*

---

*The image of the historian-as-bone-collector and restorer of human dust is found in Hammann and Herder. Despite his declarations on History-as-Resurrection, Michelet preferred, to Ezekiel's metaphor, that of Oedipus.

are false deaths, apparent deaths, half deaths, neither death nor life, and these are the worst, for they cannot enter into the historian's resurrectional system.

Michelet always had a panic terror of such death-as-sleep; not only for his own family, whose death he has always verified by systematic scarifications and obsessive exhumations,* but also for the objects of History, whose subsidence into sleep he always describes as an irremissible death, to the very degree where the motionless escapes transmutation (the corruption of corpses, a favorite theme, "too-alluring subject"). The sleep of Rome, that of Provence, even that of Christianity—so many phenomena lost to History. To these sinister torpors, Michelet opposes the frank deaths of India and of Egypt—honest deaths, "at peace and resting in their graves"—legible deaths, the regular nutriment of the historian.

SOLAR DEATH *Here, then, on one side is death-as-sleep, which stupefies the sites and clogs the sense of history, and, on the other, death-as-clarity, which floods the historical object with the very evidence of its signification. Michelet is said to have desired this death-as-sun for himself and wanted his own body, upon his death, to be exposed to the sun until dissolution. This wish has been compared to Goethe's last words:* mehr licht. *Yet this desire for a solar death had nothing aesthetic or even mythic about it. Michelet could only demand an open death, i.e., a total death: this dead historian could seek no other paradise than history itself.*

We know that such a death was in part stolen from Michelet:

*Michelet lived obsessed by the fear of a premature burial: he had the coffins of his first wife and of his father reopened, the body of his Uncle Narcisse scarified. A period obsession? A former fellow student of Michelet's, Monseigneur Allou, Bishop of Meaux, has Bossuet formally exhumed (in 1854). In 1866, Cardinal Bouvet addresses a petition to the Senate concerning apparent death: as a young man, having fallen into a cataleptic fit in the middle of a sermon, he had very nearly been buried alive.

Michelet's gràve at Père-Lachaise

not only is his wish, apparently, apocryphal, but instead of the grave of flaming sunshine which he was to have at Hyères, Michelet's widow chose to give him an official and elaborate mausoleum at Père-Lachaise. Here Jules Ferry spoke a now-forgotten oration: the radical-socialist subsidence into sleep was beginning, and Michelet entered into that motionless enchantment of which he had always been so afraid.

A MORPHOLOGY OF TISSUES   *The corruption of bodies is a pledge of their resurrection. Hence, the goal of history is to rediscover in each piece of the past's flesh the corruptible element par excellence, not the skeleton but the tissue. Michelet's anthropology is an anthropology of humors, not of forms.* In historical man, we proceed to the most fragile, we leave the expression, the features, and rediscover the corruptible and mortal substance, the color of the blood, the density of the tissues, the texture of the skin, everything which will collapse and subside in the coffin. Let us not expect to find in Michelet's Robespierre or Napoleon men-as-principles: that would be to grant too much to their immortality. In order to be the prey of History, these men must die, and even in their lives they must be marked with an essential and fragile quality, of an entirely sanguine humor, i.e., a humor liable to deterioration, already funereal. All history depends in the last instance upon the human body.†*

WHEAT-AS-FLINT   *Doomed to decomposition, the body of Micheletist man abides only because it is itself a collection of*

---

*Michelet wrote nothing about anyone without consulting as many portraits and engravings as he could. All his life he conducted a systematic interrogation of the faces he passed.

† "The first presupposition of all human history is naturally the existence of individual living beings. The first state of things to describe, then, is the corporeal organization of these individuals and the relation this gives them with all nature."
—Marx, *The German Ideology*

elementary substances. In other words, Micheletist man is perishable insofar as he is a well-fed *man. Alimentation ends by occupying in Michelet the place of all other causalities.* To compare civilizations is to compare dietetics, to contrast for instance the potbellies of Louis-Philippe and the fops of Louis Bonaparte (theme of the empty swelling) with the dry, lively man, the coffee drinker of the eighteenth century (a century favored above all others, as we know).*

Notice that we are concerned here with a new equational procedure: the national genius is nothing other than a "transformation" of the national soil. For example: the Frenchman eats bread, bread is made of wheat, wheat is merely transformed flint; thus, the Frenchman has the acute resistance of the pebble. Moist England produces grass; grass produces mutton, on which the Englishman is fed: the meat-eating British are proud and choleric yet born of a vegetal humus; their pride has something moist and swollen about it, quite remote from the Frenchman's mineral dryness: the British infants and wives, overfed Pamelas, are pale pink blossoms, milky and full-blooded, plethoric and ephemeral.

Whatever discredit Michelet attaches to certain substances, like motionless blood or waxiness, it is certain that this alimentary transmutation does not alienate him from a "full" universe, where everything is fed on everything, grass on mist, sheep on grass, and man on blood. The carnal specialty of a people or of a man can be irreplaceable (and must be, for death to have a meaning), it is nonetheless familiar. Flesh is unique, but it is not supernatural, since it is ultimately only an equality of earth, of grass, or of water. What Michelet calls "the mystery of actual and special existence," † which is the irreducible quality of a body, has noth-

---

*Feuerbach, apropos of Ireland: the blood of the potatoes, *trage Kartoffelblut,* can no longer create a revolution.
†Cf. the ideas of Cabanis and of Maine de Biran on the role of internal impressions.

The pink and milky Englishman: Pitt
"He is red . . . he is a little vulgar . . . everywhere this countenance
betrays a certain swollen, choleric childishness . . . He had a Tartuffe
mask, pink and mottled." —*Le XIXe siècle,* II, 1

ing ineffable about it, and Michelet feels justified in unifying each character of his history under a singular humor—irreplaceable no doubt, but not indescribable.

ROBESPIERRE-AS-CAT, MARAT-AS-TOAD   *The Miche-
letist portrait is different from the classical portrait in that it
describes a complexion and not an anatomy. Michelet has produced his own anti-portrait by copying out the description of
Francis of Assisi by his disciple Thomas Cellano. Here the man
is nothing but a collection of organs, appendages, and measure-
ments; he lacks, in Michelet's eyes, the living blood, the humor.
The classical portrait accumulates adjectives, it presumes there is
an infinite number of them*; Michelet's adjective is unique, it
accounts for a touch, for an ideal palpation which has found out
the body's elemental substance and no longer conceives man under any other qualification, in the fashion of a natural epithet.
Michelet says: the dry Louis XV, the cold Sieyès, and by these
denominations commits his own judgment as to the various essential movements of substance: liquefaction, viscosity, emptiness,
dryness, electricity.*

*For example, Robespierre and Charette are cats, their unity is
of a galvanic order. John Law, with his unbuttoned, splendid
throat, is entirely subject to the sign of femininity, so as to seduce
the virilized speculating women ("the viragos of the Bourse").
Marat is of the batrachian type; he is disgusting as a figure of
the fat and the icy. Vendôme is spongy, swept into the disgust of
the soaked, the stagnant. Louis XIV, whose black blood is rotten
with pungent flatulence, participates in the theme of the muddy.
Louis XVI, pale and swollen, in that of the insipid and flaccid
suet. Napoleon, yellow, waxy, and without eyebrows, induces
terror and nausea.*

---

*Balzac called for a medicine of humors *(La messe de l'Athée),* but his portraits
remain purely anatomical.

Louis XVI, a fat, pale king

Other examples of fatness: the sugary ("Mama" Toulouse, who initiated the dry Louis XV on a staircase) and the buttery (the wife of Philip V, a plump Lombard "overflowing with butter and Parmesan"). Madame de Pompadour, insipid, soft, whitish, diluted, discolors everything, like soured cream or plaster. Sade, born at Chantilly, the realm of the Condé family, derives a sinister enchantment from the place; he belongs to the "bird of prey" complexion. Catherine of Russia is minotaurian, lubricious, and bovine. Francis II (of Austria), pink and petrified, belongs to minerality. Choiseul, insolent and feminine, is a lapdog. The Duchess of Orléans (wife of the Regent), indolent and plump, emerges from the sleeping waters, of the paludal order.

NAUSEAS   *Thus, each body of the Micheletist order bears the emblem of its own flesh. The historical being has virtually no psychology; rather, he is reduced to a sole substance, and if he is condemned, it is not by the judgment of his motives or his actions, but by virtue of the quality of attraction or repulsion attached to his flesh. For Michelet, the human body is only a humor, and this humor is never neutral, it does not fail to commit the historian to an impulse of effusion or of disgust. In the order of substance, it is motionless fluid which most disgusts Michelet, whence a special nausea confronting the stagnant and the icy: in the order of animality (so fecund in disgusts), it is felinity and reptility, i.e., the electric and the greasy.*

Thus, the human body is entirely an immediate judgment, but its value is of an existential and not intellectual order. Michelet condemns by virtue of his nauseas, not of his principles. Michelet doubtless had good reasons—biographical or ideological—for detesting the Empire or the Monarchy; but these reasons were those of thousands of his contemporaries; the rejection of autocracy became a Micheletist phenomenon only on the level of existence, not on that of ideas: the Monarchy being a swelling

Marie-Victoire Sophie de Noailles, Comtesse de Toulouse
"Ripe, pious, sugary, still fresh, plump and lovely, this lady had the privilege of reassuring and even attracting a very timid king."
— *Histoire de France,* XVI, 2

Woman-as-Minotaur:
Catherine of Russia

La Duchess d'Orléans
"With her thick, drawling speech,
with her great indolence, she seemed
a stagnant pool, a kind of sinister swamp."
—*Histoire de France,* XIV, 18

and the Empire a waxiness, reprobation turned to nausea. Michelet's kings and queens thus form a veritable pharmacy of disgust. They are not condemned, they are loathed.

It is evident that Micheletist man needs no personal psychology; he has none but that of Michelet himself: kings, queens, soldiers, ministers, ancient gods, and women of the people—all the population of history speaks the language of Michelet's father, a journeyman printer, a former guard of the Temple, etc., or that of Michelet and his wife Athénaïs. Consider the Micheletist version of the Song of Songs (in La bible de l'humanité): the encounter of the Bridegroom and the Bride (mystic or not, it matters little here) is indulgently described as a sentimental adventure of the silliest sort, a naïvely licentious best-seller of the Georges Ohnet variety. This is because psychology, detached from the Humor, is nothing but mechanics; strip the characters of their bodies, and they have no further identity; you can inveterately assign them the same language, the same interior, the same conjugal behavior, which will necessarily be those of Michelet himself. Strip Michelet of his existential thematics, he remains no more than a petit-bourgeois.

ROSE AND BULL Indeed, the opacity of their flesh absorbs the entire social life of the Micheletist creatures. In a naïvely bourgeois décor, they live together only on the level of the greatest erotic or passional nervosity: incestuous relations (Nero, François I, Louis XV, the Regent, Napoleon), Louis XIII's exasperation with the jolly Anne of Austria, conquest of Louis XIV by the mischievous Duchess of Burgundy, lesbianism of Sarah Marlborough and Queen Anne, coquetry of Mirabeau and Marie-Antoinette—so many situations in which it is complexions which attract or confront each other, not characters. The great historical situations, which would give birth in a painter to a genre picture, are always in Michelet a kind of electric conflagration, one born from the contact of chemically antipathetic bodies.

Such is the crumpling of the Rose by the Bull (we are to understand, the marriage of Marie-Louise to Napoleon), or the confrontation of the (electric) dry and the (feminine) full in the death of Robespierre. This long historical scene is organized in Michelet like an act of pure carnal humiliation, that of a cold man half undone in the filthy sheets, jaw pendulous, and watched *by opulent women, crimson in velvet, well-fed, and jubilant, i.e., sterility itself exposed and sold to triumphant warmth.*

RIDDLE-PORTRAITS *It is only when provided with their humor that the characters glimpsed in history, living then with all the disgust—or with some more ambiguous sentiment, such as erotic pity—which they provoke, can be both event and value, history and its moral. As we have just seen, Napoleon's waxiness, Louis XIV's materiality, Louis XVI's flaccidity involve a general discredit of monarchic government. But more profoundly, it is by a hidden interplay of associations that the humor receives its ethic. For example, Napoleon's stoutness makes him, at the end, a phantasmagorical figure. Now, we must recall that phantas-magoria is linked to a particularly maleficent Micheletist theme, that of the Lottery, of Gambling. Bonaparte, already doomed to fortune by the occult destination of his name, is then discredited less as a tyrant than as an actor, an illusionist (a Jupiter-as-Scarpin). Madame de Maintenon, desexed or bisexed, at once the king's preacher and his mistress, dressed in black and holding a rose, participates in the theme of the Suspect, the Equivocal.*

Hence, there is a hermeneutics of the Micheletist portrait, because each body is a secret, and because, in History, this secret is frozen, each character capable of being only for a moment eternalized in flesh and in action. The action "surprised" is in effect a necessary dimension to the representation of the human body in History. We see this in all historical painting, which is impossible without a certain solemnity. In Michelet, this posture is not decorative at all, as it is for instance in a painter of the Empire. The royal bodies are always rendered with triviality, those of the women quite greedily. But the rhetoric necessary to all historical painting is not necessarily noble; what matters is that the man of History be presented in an amplified gesture, struck by an enchantment which transmits him through Time, neither living nor dead, in a third state of dreamed existence which enlarges and imposes *him. However defective Michelet's Napoleon, he is of the same substance as the Napoleon of Baron Gros, for instance: both have that unreal fleshiness of the heroized man; their immobility* in front of *the historian or in front of the painter holds captive a* gestuary, *a style of action: History is founded.*

Dry death: the Cannon of Mahomet II *(Dürer)*

To Monsieur Taine, rue [du] Dragon   [no date; *c.* 1855]

Monsieur,

You have covered me with praise as a *writer,* and your article is very strong and very serious, except that in one sense it is partial.

New as you are to criticism, you are as yet unaware that this name of *poet* which you apply to me is precisely the accusation by which the historian is always dogged. This word is responsible for the worst abuses.

I have made every effort to give history a serious and positive basis at an infinity of points. Examples: the history of the bank (in my book on the Reformation), the budget of King Philip (in the wars of religion, etc.). The election of Charles V, treated politically by Mignet, has been treated *financially* by me, that is, in terms of its truth.

Yet everywhere people have written that I was a historian of *a fortunate imagination.*

I greet you cordially, and ask you to accept my gratitude.

J. Michelet

—Quoted in J.-M. Carré, *Michelet et son temps*

I acknowledge that this history is not impartial. It does not maintain a discreet and prudent equilibrium between good and evil. On the contrary, it is partial, frankly and vigorously so, in behalf of what is true and right. If one line should be found in which the author has attenuated, weakened the narratives or the judgments out of regard for a certain opinion, a certain power, he would wish to strike out the entire text.

"Then you mean," it will be said, "that no one else is sincere? Do you claim for yourself a monopoly of honesty?" Such is not my thought. I shall merely say that the most honorable have kept the respect for certain things and for certain men, and that, on the contrary, history, which is the world's judge, has as its first duty to lose such respect.

A fine judge, one who would take off his hat to everyone brought before his tribunal! Rather, they must stand bareheaded and answer when history interrogates them; and I say, to all of them: all stand before judgment, men and ideas, kings, laws, peoples, dogmas and philosophies.

Hence, no concession, no conciliatory arrangements, and no compromise. No indulgence in order to inflect law to fact, or to soften fact and bring it into accord with law.

That, in the sum of centuries and in the total harmony of humanity's life, fact and law ultimately coincide, I do not doubt. But to put in the detail, in the battle, this fatal opium of the philosophy of history, these manipulations of a false peace, is to put death into life, is to kill both history and morality, is to ask the indifferent soul: "Who is bad, who is good?"

I have expressed the morality of my work.

But what is that morality from the point of view of the art of history? What does it seek? What does the author claim?

Only one thing.

Many subjects had been illuminated, many works existed on this or that part of the sixteenth century. Several features of this century had been noted, several aspects discussed. And the countenance of the century remained hidden; it had not been seen (in the ensemble) by any eye as yet.

I believe I have seen this century full in the face, and I have tried to reveal what I have seen. At the least, I have given a true impression of its physiognomy.

1856. *Histoire de France,* X, Conclusion

THE BENCH OF HISTORY

Each soul, among vulgar things, possesses certain special, individual aspects which do not come down to the same thing, and which must be noted when this soul passes and proceeds into the unknown world.

Suppose we were to constitute a guardian of graves, a kind of tutor and protector of the dead?

I have spoken elsewhere of the duty which concerned Camoëns on the deadly shores of India: *administrator of the property of the deceased.*

Yes, each dead man leaves a small property, his memory, and asks that it be cared for. For the one who has no friends, the magistrate must supply one. For the law, for justice is more reliable than all our forgetful affections, our tears so quickly dried.

This magistracy is History. And the dead are, to speak in the fashion of Roman Law, those *miserabiles personae* with whom the magistrate must be concerned.

Never in my career have I lost sight of that duty of the Historian. I have given many of the too-forgotten dead the assistance which I myself shall require.

I have exhumed them for a second life. Some were not

born at a moment suitable to them. Others were born on the eve of new and striking circumstances which have come to erase them, so to speak, stifling their memory (example, the Protestant heroes dead before the brilliant and forgetful epoch of the eighteenth century, the age of Montesquieu and of Voltaire).

History greets and renews these disinherited glories; it gives life to these dead men, resuscitates them. Its justice thus associates those who have not lived at the same time, offers reparation to some who appeared so briefly only to vanish. Now they live with us, and we feel we are their relatives, their friends. Thus is constituted a family, a city shared by the living and the dead.

1872. *Histoire du XIXe siècle,* II, *Le Directoire*, Preface

OEDIPUS

The historian is neither Caesar nor Claudius, but he often sees in his dreams a weeping, lamenting crowd, the host of those who have not lived enough, who wish to live again . . . It is not only an urn and tears which these dead ask of you. It is not enough for them that we take their sighs upon ourselves. It is not a mourner they would have, it is a sooth-sayer, a *vates.* So long as they have no such person, they will wander about their ill-sealed graves and find no rest.

They must have an Oedipus who will explain to them their own enigma, of which they have not had the meaning, who will teach them what their words, their acts meant, which they did not understand. They must have a Prome-theus, so that, at the fire he has stolen, the voices which floated like snowflakes in the air might rebel, might produce a sound, might begin to speak. There must be more; the words must be heard which were never spoken, which remained deep in their hearts (search your own, they are there); the silences of history must be made to speak, those terrible pedal points in which history says nothing more, and which are precisely its most tragic accents. Then only will the dead be resigned to the sepulcher. They are beginning to understand their destiny, to restore the dissonances to a sweeter harmony, to say among themselves, and in a whisper, the last words of Oedipus: Remember me. The shades greet each other and subside in peace. They let their urns be sealed again. They scatter, lulled by friendly hands, fall back to sleep and renounce their dreams. That precious urn of bygone times—the pontiffs of history bear it and transmit it to each other with what piety, what tender care! (no one knows how pious but themselves), as they would bear the ashes of their father or of their son. Their son? But is it not themselves?

1842. Quoted in Monod, *Vie et pensée de Michelet,* II, 6

IRREPLACEABLE MAN

[*Death of the Duc d'Orléans, assassinated by the Burgundians*]
And everyone wept, enemies and friends alike. There were no longer enemies then; each man, at those moments, becomes a partisan of the dead man. So young, so vital just now, and already gone! Beauty, grace, chivalry, a beacon of knowledge, a sweet and lively speaker—yesterday all that, today nothing . . .

Nothing? . . . More, perhaps. The man who yesterday seemed a mere individual—one sees that he had within himself more than one existence, that he was indeed a multiple being, infinitely varied! . . . Admirable virtue of death! Only death reveals life. The living man is seen by each of us only from one side, as he serves or hampers us. He dies, and then we see him from a thousand new aspects, we distinguish all the various links that bound him to the world. Thus, when you strip the ivy from the oak which supported it, you perceive underneath countless living threads which you could never separate from the bark where they lived; they will remain broken, yet they will remain.

Each man is a humanity, a universal history . . . And yet this being, in whom abided an infinite generality, was at the same time a special individual, a person, a unique, irreparable being whom nothing will replace. Nothing of the kind before, nothing after; God will not begin again. Others will come, no doubt; the world, which is inexhaustible, will bring to life other persons, better ones perhaps, but the same as this? Never, never . . .

1840. *Histoire de France,* IV, 1

WHEAT-AS-FLINT

History always tells us how we die, never how we live.

Yet each people has a special nutriment which engenders it day by day, so to speak, and is its quotidian creator.

For the French, from time immemorial, it is bread, and soup. For the English, especially since 1760 and the discoveries of Backwell, who invented new breeds of cattle, that nutriment is chiefly meat.

Forced to labor, to travel, England has increasingly committed herself to meat, has made a religion of it, so to speak. The child fed, to the age of twelve, on meat grows enormously and assumes all the luster of the rose.

Yet, amid this fortifying diet, England confessed fatigue, inveterately cried: "Bread!" until the laws of Robert Peel brought the country the grains of France, Russia, Poland, etc.

A curious thing: France, after so many deadly adventures, having lost so much blood, had not grown too thin to offer food to England.

Albion claimed that the very stature of the French had diminished. A possibility, after Bonaparte. Yet the race remained stronger than ever. The undernourished peasant, it was said, sufficed for the hardest labor. One sees how substantial a nourishment is wheat, though it does not afford, like meat, the energy of the moment. This wheat, ultimately, is the flint which infiltrates into the blossoming plant and gives it a persistence, a singular duration of nutritive powers.

France, let it be known, is fed on stone. This diet gives her, at moments, her spark of life, and in her bones a great power of resistance.

1872. *Histoire du XIXe siècle,* III, *Waterloo,* Preface

AN ANTI-MICHELETIST PORTRAIT: THOMAS CELLANO'S FRANCIS OF ASSISI

"A round head, low forehead, ingenuous black eyes, straight brows, a fine straight nose, tiny alert ears, a sharp-pointed tongue, a gentle but emphatic voice; close-set, regular white teeth; thin lips, scanty beard, skinny neck, short arms, long fingers and nails, slender legs, tiny feet, and no apparent fleshiness."

1833. *Histoire de France* II, 8

THE FEMININITY OF JOHN LAW

At this time, all Europe was infected with speculation fever. Quite mistakenly, the other nations looked down on us, prided themselves on their invulnerability, mocked us with the folly

Mr. JEAN LAW. Cõnseiller du Roy
en tous Ses conseils directeur general de la
Banque Royale cy devant Controleur
general des Finances.

LAW. cet heureux genie c'est donne a la France
dans l'affreux Embaras ou etoit cet etat
le Soin qu'il prend d'aranger la finance
va rendre aux françois l'abondance et l'Eclat.

Paris Chez L. Crepy rue St Jacques vis avis la rue du Platre of Law's *System*. The same folly was in them, but hardly of an amusing sort: there was neither wit nor system there. There was simply avarice.

Three and four times England and sober Holland suffered such seizures. But, in analogous form, the idea, the goal were contrary. What did they seek by such profits? To hoard. The French, to expend, to live the good life, amusement, society.

Add gaming for gaming's sake, the lure of combat, the joy of that skirmish, the vanity of saying: "I am lucky, I am blessed, I am the son of Fortune! It is my lot! *I was born with a caul!*"

If anyone was entitled to say such a thing, it was John Law, for certain. He was much handsomer than a man should be: elegant, delicate, with that gentle beauty which suited this era when women prevailed in all things. It was for them, certainly—for the mob of lovely gamesters who were mad for him—that his first portrait was made. At this time he has only a minor title, *conseiller du roi;* he is still a beginner, in his rising period. His is the dawn and hope, Fortune herself, in a very feminine aspect, with her promises and her dreams of pleasure and agreeable vice. An indecent image, in all conscience, his neck and chest bare, devised to flatter virile loves, the masculine penchants of those frenzied bacchantes of the Bourse, who knows? to rush them into the purchase of shares?

1863. *Histoire de France,* XV, 7

MARAT-AS-TOAD

Caught this way in this shout of murder, and as if with his hand still bloodied, Marat should have been thunderstruck. Far from it. He who had always hidden himself appeared

happy to show himself in broad daylight: boldly he accepted the light and the challenge. The creature of darkness came out to display himself in the sun, smiling with that wide mouth of his, seeming to say to those who (like Madame Roland) doubted if Marat was a real being: "You doubted? Lo and behold!"

His mere presence on the tribunal roused everyone: the place seemed corrupted by it. His broad low figure which scarcely went beyond the head and chest and spread sideways, those plump, heavy hands which he lay on the witness stand, those bulging eyes, gave no notion of a man, but rather of a toad . . .

1850. *Histoire de la Révolution,* IV, 3

SPONGY VENDÔME

At the Château d'Eu, a large equestrian portrait shows the man himself. He has mounted the first horse he could find, a good, heavy black horse which a blacksmith had given him, in default of his own, to charge into battle: a heavy Spanish mount, with a glowing eye, strong and responsive to pulls at the bit. He himself is pasty-faced, evidently unhealthy. The face has some relation with the swollen and depraved mask of Mirabeau (in the Saint-Albin Museum). Both, from their Italian blood, had a tendency to farce and to the sublime. In Vendôme, the odd gaze also recalls the Gascon side and the Béarnais trickster. All in all, he is an old child, a chubby baby of fifty-six. One might laugh; but something troubles and confuses the mind: the riddle of a spongy, pug nose, a wretched affliction which did not come from Mars. The Spaniards, who were very fond of him, after his battle of Villaviciosa, characterized him on his triumphal procession with a charming word. All Madrid shouted: "Cupidón!"

1862. *Histoire de France,* XIV, 2

I know only two faithful portraits of Napoleon. One is Houdon's little bust (1800), fierce, dim, and shadowy, which seems
a sinister enigma. The other is a painting which represents
him at full length in his study (1810?), a work by David,
who, it is said, spent two years on it and here showed himself conscientious, brave, and without concern to flatter, con-
centrating only on truth. So much so that the engraver
(Grignon) did not dare to follow him in certain details, in
which the truth ran counter to tradition. David showed him
as he always was, without lashes or eyebrows, with very
little hair, and that of a nondescript chestnut color, which in
his youth seemed black by dint of pomade.

The gray eyes—like a pane of glass through which one
sees nothing. Finally, a complete impersonality, so obscure
as to seem phantasmagorical.

He is plump, and yet one distinguishes the feature which
he had from birth, and which he inherited from his mother:
very prominent cheekbones, common among Corsicans and
Sardinians. He himself said that he resembled her and took
after her in everything. In his youth, he was her shrunken,
diminished image. If you put the picture of his mother beside this, this one seems a desiccated imitation of it, as if the
hereditary disease in the family, cancer of the stomach, had
already begun gnawing at him from within.

On the contrary, Madame Laetitia, in her Italian portraits,
like the one before me as I write, is of an imposing beauty.
She has an indefinable, mysterious, tragic quality. You cannot take your eyes from her. The hostile, disdainful mouth
is full of that bitter honey found only in Corsica. The fixed,
black eyes, very wide open, are no less enigmatic for that. If

Bonaparte, *by Houdon*

they stare, it is within, at their dream or their passion. This gives her the strange look of a fortuneteller, or of a Moorish sibyl, descended from the Carthaginians or the Saracens, whose graves are found near Ajaccio and whose posterity still exists in the Niolo. She has the dark air of a prophetess of doom, or of those *voceratrices* who follow funerals, not with tears but rather with imprecations of vengeance.

1872. *Histoire du XIXe siècle,* I, iii, 1

ROSE AND BULL

[Marriage of Napoleon and Marie-Louise]
This was a human sacrifice. Marie-Louise, for all her rosy luster and the freshness of a girl of twenty, was like a dead woman. She was handed over to the Minotaur, to the great enemy of her family, to the murderer of the Duke d'Enghien. Would he not devour her? . . . His yellow Corsican skin had acquired, with its fat, a whitish, quite phantasmagorical tinge. The daughter of the north, a rose (a rather vulgar rose, as Prudhon has painted her), was terrified of the contact.

1872. *Histoire du XIXe siècle,* III, *Waterloo,* iv, 8

THE DEATH OF ROBESPIERRE

Between five and six occurred, in the slow and lugubrious promenade of the carts through the narrow rue Saint-Denis, through the rue de la Ferronnerie, down the whole length of the rue Saint-Honoré, the hideous exhibition.

Hideous in several senses. There were dead and dying men, miserable bleeding bodies handed over to the joys of the mob. To make them stand on their feet, they were bound with ropes to the rails of the carts, their legs, arms and heads

Robespierre-as-Cat

wagging. The jolts of the rough pavements of Paris must have shocked them at every step of the way.

Robespierre, head wrapped in a filthy bloodstained rag which bound up his dislocated jaw, in that horrible situation which no defeated man had ever endured—bearing the dread weight of a whole people's curse—kept his stiff posture, his firm bearing, his dry, fixed gaze. His intelligence was integral, soaring above his situation and doubtless disentangling the true from the false in the furies that were pursuing him.

The tide of reaction rose so fast and so powerfully that the Committees decided to triple the guards around the prisons. All along the route of the condemned crowded those who claimed to be relatives of the victims of the Terror, to howl at Robespierre, to play in this melancholy ceremony the chorus of ancient vengeance. This false tragedy around the true one, this concert of calculated shouts, of premeditated frenzies, was the first scene of the white Terror.

The horrible thing was the windows, rented at fantastic prices. Unknown faces, which had long been concealed, emerged into daylight. A world of rich men and young beauties paraded on these balconies. Taking advantage of this violent reaction of public sensibility, their fierce rage dared show itself. The women especially offered an intolerable spectacle. Impudent, half naked on the excuse of the July weather, breasts covered with flowers, resting their elbows on velvet cloths, leaning out into the rue Saint-Honoré, with the men behind them, they screamed in shrill voices: "To death! To the guillotine!" Boldly that day they resumed their elaborate gowns, and that evening they *supped*. No one showed any further constraint. Sade came out of prison on 10 Thermidor.

The scaffold gendarmes, who the night before, in the Faubourg, under Henriot's orders, dispersed with saber blows those who had shouted "Pardon!," today fawned on the new power, and, with the points of their sabers beneath the chins of the condemned, displayed them to the curious: "Here he is, that famous Couthon! Now have a look at your Robespierre!"

Nothing was spared them. Having reached the Church of the Assumption, in front of the Maison Duplay, the actors played out a scene. Furies danced round them in a circle. A child was there on the spot, with a bucket of ox blood; with a broom, he flung drops against the wall of the house. Robespierre closed his eyes.

That evening, these same bacchantes rushed to Sainte-Pélagie, where Mère Duplay was, shouting that they were the widows of Robespierre's victims. They made the terrified jailers open the doors, strangled the old woman, and hanged her from her own curtain rod.

Robespierre had drunk with wormwood all that the world contains. At last he reached the gateway, the Place de la Révolution. He mounted the steps of the scaffold with a steady tread. All, in the same way, showed themselves calm, strong in their intention, in their ardent patriotism, and in their sincerity. Saint-Just had long since embraced death and the future. He died worthy, grave, and simple. France will never be consoled for such a hope; this man was great with a greatness that was his own, owing nothing to fortune, and he alone would have been strong enough to make the sword tremble before the Law.

Must a vile thing be said? A servant of the guillotine and a cowardly flatterer of the mob (was it the same man who slapped Charlotte Corday?), seeing this frenzy in the place, this passion of vengeance against Robespierre, suddenly yanked away the bandage holding the dislocated jaw . . . Robespierre uttered one groan . . . He was seen for a moment dead white, hideous, mouth wide open and his broken teeth falling out . . . Then there was a muffled thud . . . This great man was no more.

Twenty-one tormented victims, few enough for the mob which thirsted for blood and would have it. The next day it was regaled with all the blood of the Commune: seventy heads at once! And for dessert at this banquet, twelve heads on the third day.

We may note that, of these hundred persons, half were entirely unknown to Robespierre, and had never figured save in name in the Commune.

Let us draw breath and avert our eyes. "Sufficient unto the day is the suffering thereof." We have no need to tell here what followed, the blind reaction that swept the Assembly and from which it emerged only by Vendémiaire. Here horror and absurdity fought it out on an equal footing. The silliness of Lecointre, the inept rage of the Frérons, the mercenary perfidy of the Talliens, encouraging the most cowardly, an execrable farce begun, lucrative murders in the name of humanity, the vengeance of *sensitive men* massacring the patriots and continuing their work, the purchase of national property. The *black band* wept hot tears for relatives it had never had, cut its rivals' throats, and got illicit glimpses of the decrees in order to buy in secret.

Paris once again became very gay. There was famine, it was true, but the promenades were radiant, the Palais-Royal was full, the theaters packed. Then began those *bals des victimes,* in which an impudent luxury displayed itself in an orgy of false grief.

By this path, we proceeded to the great tomb in which France has sealed five million men.

A few days after Thermidor, a man, alive today, who was then ten years of age, was taken to the theater by his parents, and, on leaving, admired the long row of gleaming carriages which met his eyes for the first time. People in livery, sweeping off their caps, were saying to the spectators as they left the theater: "Is a carriage required, *mon maître?*" The child was not certain what these new words meant. He had them explained to him, and was merely told that there had been a great change brought about by the death of Robespierre.

1853. Histoire de la Révolution, VII, xx, 10

Nous avons commencé
à vous lire, cher ami, en
pleurant de joie. Nous avons
lu la représentation d'hier.
tout cela est d'une
simplicité grande et forte qui
va au cœur.

je vous en prie, faites une table.
Il en est temps encore
    je vous embrasse de cœur. Ma
femme vous félicite, ainsi que madame
Noël.   J. Michelet

Dans ce mois, la Réforme

Le Si

FLOWER OF BLOOD

For Michelet, Blood is the cardinal substance of History. Consider Robespierre's death, for example: here two bloods confront each other: one poor, dry, so meager that it requires the aid of an artificial blood, galvanic power; the other, that of the women of Thermidor (the solar month of history), a superlative blood which unites the characteristics of a superb sanguinity: the hot, the red, the naked, the overfed. These two bloods are in opposition. And then the Woman-as-Blood devours the Priest-as-Cat.

MILKY WATER, SANDY WATER *Before Blood, there is water. Take Germany, for instance; we must distinguish two time sequences in the genetics of this country: a first Germany, "pale, vague, indecisive, a child-world," then a new Germany, full of sanguinary power, great and fecund, "the womb and brain of Europe." By which we are to understand that the age of water, which is only a vague and risky fecundity, has given way to a sort of sanguinary fixation; Germany promoted to the rank of womb (the bloodiest organ possible, of which Michelet has several times given enthusiastic descriptions), which means that Germany-as-Woman, hence sovereignly beneficent, has replaced her aquatic, drifting origins with a truly adult blood, inured to crises and to repose.*

In contrast, you have Russia, a shapeless world which has

always remained in a state of drifting, evasive, undivided water, unable to achieve the personality of Blood: the Russians are not yet men. This is because the primal water is not, here, as in the case of Germany, that liquid and free element, beneficent and milky, which could be changed into blood. A substance always prevents it: mud. The Russian Empire is not made of a mobile water, but of a sandy, deceptive, ever-sleeping water: Bismarck (not German at all, but Prussian, i.e., Slavic), from the abandoned sands of the Baltic, and Napoleon III (from the gray waters of Holland, from its dubious and leaden soil), these are the encounter of two sterilities of the same substance, and this substance is motionless water, water without a regular flux, caricature and negation of blood.

BLOOD-AS-CORPSE   *There is in Michelet a primary horror of clotted blood, of blood-as-corpse. Dead blood thickens and cakes, it is drawn into the disgust of the fat and the greasy. At Versailles, from an airy loggia, the lovely ladies came to watch the* curée *of the stags. Here we are to understand that two ignoble bloods are in confrontation: the triumphant, plethoric blood of the opulent aristocrat (prefiguration of the Thermidorian woman who also leaned on a balcony to see Robespierre led to the* curée*) and the sticky blood of the murdered animal. A disgust not at all metaphorical, since Michelet would have much preferred to be a vegetarian (and if he was not, it was because he believed that meat was necessary for work). To the Hindu, weak, feminine, and fruit-eating, he contrasts with disgust the overfed European, "doubling the strength of his race by that semi-intoxication which is the inveterate condition of these swallowers of meat and blood."* *

---

* So far as I know, no one has paid much attention to Michelet's Brahmanism. Yet the father of his second wife (Athénaïs, an initiatic name if ever there was one) was a vegetarian, a bird tamer. It was after his second marriage that Michelet's Hinduism ceases to be bookish (Burnouf, Anquetil) and becomes militant.

THE SANGUINARY PLETHORA *Motionless blood generates two nauseas: that of engorged blood, of the sanguinary plethora, and that of icy blood, pale and hardened. England is discredited by her meat diet, by that voration of opaque blood, of blood-as-flesh, of solidified blood, which produces the proud and the choleric. (We are to understand that pride is a sin only insofar as it constitutes a kind of stasis of the blood, a terrific coagulation of the sanguinary rhythm.) The British virgin disgusts because she consists entirely of sleeping blood derived from meats and liquors (narcotic theme).*

The same disgust for Marie Alacoque, foundress of the Sacred Heart, born in vinous Burgundy and engorged on a plethoric blood, from which the Jesuits have derived the insipid and nauseating image of the Bleeding Heart of Jesus. Another sanguinary plethora: that of Marat, whose "sensibility" was nothing but a mist of blood, a woman's mutability, and who had to be "disgorged" by regular bleedings.

BLUE BLOOD *On the contrary, but quite as discredited, is white blood hard as ice. This is chiefly a virginal blood, the humor of any being which has not acceded to fecundity (or to pity). Thus, history offers Michelet two terrible virgins, and these virgins are men: Charles XII (of Sweden) and Saint-Just. The mixture of blue (mineral) eyes and of transparent (aquatic) skin which constitutes them involves them both in a sort of abortive, monstrous femininity. These two "virgins of Tauris," whose motionless and inhuman blood seems dedicated to sacred murder, participate in the horror of the raw, of the icy, of sterile azure and mutilating steel.*

WHITE BLOOD *Other forms of white blood: first of all, insipid blood, that of Robespierre, the bloodless phrasemaker, who* delights the bloodthirsty women before being devoured by them. Then old, soft blood, that of degeneration, pale to the point of dryness: blood of Caesar, extenuated by debauchery, a pale figure shown crossing the marshes of Gaul, and scarcely to be distinguished from them; blood of Alexander, a barbarian not a Greek, a true Nordic blood, moist, foggy, bewildered, likely to become the archetype of all crazed monarchic turgidities.

CRAZED BLOOD AND SEALED BLOOD   *Indeed, blood is a witness-substance, before which all History comes to judgment. Whatever does not participate in its redeeming quality, which is rhythm, lapses into a discredited history (i.e., nausea). Sanguinary efflorescence is constantly threatened by all the possible forms of disorder or decomposition. Contrasting with the hardened or engorged bloods are the furious, arhythmic, chaotic bloods, swept toward madness or corruption. Whole centuries collapse into the avatars of an unstable blood: the thirteenth into leprosy, the fourteenth into the black plague, the sixteenth into syphilis, the nineteenth into cancers of the womb. Louis XIV, paragon of monarchy, is wholly discredited by his black blood. One can say, moreover, that the kings and queens are abhorred by Michelet to the degree that their blood, sealed, is by definition motionless. Heredity in a closed circuit produces a kind of sanguinary stasis that is particularly noxious; there is a correspondence between the political malfeasance of the "family conspiracy" and the malignity of royal blood decomposed by its closure.*

All the great feudal houses, moreover, are degraded by their blood, and in a sense History is merely conflicts of sick and enraged bloods: the Burgundians have composite blood, they produce strange frenzies, suffer fits of grim madness (Charles the Bold, cross-bred, moreover, with Portuguese blood); the Anjou–Plantagenets have monstrous blood: of abnormal size (William the Conqueror could not be laid in his grave), voracious, bitter, they are Satanic, ensorcelled (here reappears the maleficent theme of the Englishman-as-Satan, Warwick for instance); the Guise–Lorraines have a complex blood, their natural element is the imbroglio, the goal almost achieved and always missed. The Valois are Saturnian and leaden. All these bloods, already doomed, can be further mixed among themselves and produce a multiplied decomposition: such as Charles V, thrice Lancastrian, product of three discords, Austrian, English, and Spanish.

ANTI-BLOODS   *There are also substances which are antipathetic to blood and which form a kind of mocking figure of it. First of these, stone, mineral; i.e., ultimately, the dry, the desert, the void. Consider Madame de Prie: at first swollen with blood by Law's System, she suddenly dries out and, when its vogue passes, shifts from blood to stone. This sort of mineral apocalypse, which lies in wait for fine fresh red blood, Michelet has moreover placed exemplarily at the heart of the most sanguinary site there is, the womb: dissecting a woman's body at Clamart, he discovers in it a calculus, blood changed to stone; whence terror and pity, all the effects of the myth.*

Another form of anti-blood: the nerves, the pale, ethereal, cerebral life of the nineteenth century, for instance, as opposed to the primitive centuries when "red" was a synonym for "fine." We have already seen apropos of Robespierre that the bloodless was identified with the galvanic; electricity is a dry caricature of the blood; it runs as blood runs, but is merely empty; blood swells, distends, dissolves, links, and its rhythmic surface traces the beneficent figure of the homogeneous. Electricity contracts and withdraws, it incinerates without fecundating. There is between felinity and Robespierre, for example, that common element which is a kind of acrid, dry fire, an eroticism sterile to the very degree that it is bloodless. Speaking of a cat he had which, while hunting Spanish flies, happened to be consumed in

Madame Roland
"She is strong and already a little motherly, serene, firm, and resolute,
with an evident critical tendency." —*La Révolution,* V, 5

this orgy of dry fire, Michelet does not fail to contrast it with the creamy and "sopitive" substance of a worm which, when eaten (all except the head), puts young Brazilian girls to sleep beneath the veil of a cool, continuous dream.

Naturally, all these substances have moral forms: the electric (identified with the cerebral) involves all its affinities in the discredit attached to the Scholastic, the Byzantine, the sophisticated; and conversely, blood glorifies the barbaric, the primitive, which does not divide but envelops.

CONJUGAL BLOOD   *Beneficent blood is mobile; it undergoes returns. To the white-skinned and blue-eyed, marmoreal and icy virgins of Tauris (Charles XII of Sweden, Saint-Just), Michelet contrasts the complexion of the woman of thirty, transparent but capable of blushing, pure and fragile beneath the periodic flush of blood ("the modest and charming blushes that so often rise to her cheeks"). He prefers the rosy white of the bride to the virid white of the virgin.* Consider the pearl: virginal whiteness? "No, better than that; virgins and little girls always have, however sweet and gentle they may be, a touch of youthful greenness about them. The pearl's candor is rather that of the innocent bride, so pure yet subject to love."*

Michelet's historical feminine repertoire consists chiefly of accomplished, almost middle-aged women, well-established in sanguinary circulation; they are all somewhat motherly, like Anne of Austria, Madame de Montespan (though charmless), or Madame Roland, all of the complexion which he calls "lilies and roses." Such women-as-flowers (who easily become women-as-fruits, ready for manducation) are quite dependent upon blood, their body is only a parasitical envelope of their own blood.

---

*Balzac's feminine repertoire is also conjugal—or para-conjugal—and not virginal.

Mlle Aissé

Anne of Austria, *by Rubens*

SIRENIC CREATURES   *This is because, for Michelet, blood is not at all a sealed biological element, strictly belonging to this or that person who possesses his blood as he might possess eyes or legs. It is a cosmic element, a unique and homogeneous substance which traverses all bodies, without losing, in this accidental individuation, anything of its universality. Itself a transformation of the earth (of bread and of the fruits that we eat), it has the immensity of an element.*

Hence, the superlative form of blood is finally the sea. The sea, which is the primordial genetic element, constitutes the archetype of blood and of milk, "the sweet milk, and the warm blood." It produces both milk and blood by a kind of progressive organization, of tumescence analogous to all the phenomena of spontaneous generation (in which Michelet firmly believed). In a free state, the sea is already a milky element by the whitish and pulpy nature of its fish. At a higher stage, it becomes blood and milk in the whale, a perfect mythic creature, "true flower of the world," "well above all earthly creation." This alliance of salt, blood, and milk defines for Michelet a substance of cosmic, almost Gnostic order, since it is at once origin and goal, element and flower. As early as 1842, at the bedside of his dying friend (Madame Dumesnil), Michelet was reading an encyclopedia article on the cetaceans and could not tear himself away from it, forgetting about the dead woman. In La mer, *the whale crowns the sequence of beings, it is a sirenic creature; in fact, it is a hypostasis of Woman, and as such liberates in Michelet all the automatisms of effusion and inclusion (which he calls Pity) functionally attached to any image of the sanguinary and lactescent woman, i.e., the woman rhythmically swollen.*

FLOWER OF BLOOD   *Blood being the terminal substance of creation, the "flower of blood" will therefore be for Michelet* the very figure of perfection. It is an object at once cosmic, aesthetic, and moral; it signifies an undivided world in which contraries are abolished.

The child, for example, who is of the same substance as the People, constitutes a kind of ideal femininity, insofar as he consists of a mixture of milk and blood, and in whom this double germinal liquor flows transparently, without ever being engorged, diluted, or dried up, quite unlike woman, sanguinary and lactescent no doubt, but threatened by plethora (Marie Alacoque), petrification (the womb producing stones), or drying up (cruel paradox of the women of 1765, who just after the publication of Émile sought to give suck to their newborn babies without sacrificing their parties). The child then is "the true flower of blood," "the dazzling and tender flower of blood," and this "thick carnal garment" in which man begins his life is merely "a heavy incarnation of thought, filled with milk, with blood, and with poetry."

Here then is another instancing of the ultimate beneficent image, of a liquid closure, cyclically refreshed by the rhythm of Nature which causes the blood to rise like flowers, like the tides.

Fluctuation: Jean Goujon

". . . The ravishing hand of Jean Goujon, who gave to stone the undulating grace, the very breath of France, who could make marble flow like our restless waters, imparting to it the fluctuation of tall ephemeral grasses and floating harvests." —*Histoire de France,* VIII, 19

Indeed, Germany is a kind of India in Europe, huge, vague, drifting, and fecund, like its God, the Proteus of pantheism. As long as Germany has not been pressed in upon and sealed off by the powerful barriers of the monarchies surrounding it, the Indo-Germanic tribe has overflowed, streamed across Europe, and changed it while changing itself. Yielded up, then, to its natural mobility, it knew neither walls nor city. "Each family," says Tacitus, "stops where its whim detains it, at a wood, a meadow, a spring." But while, behind Germany, mounted the tide of another Barbary—Slavs, Avars, and Hungarians—while, in the West, France was sealed off, it became necessary to live more densely in order not to lose land and to build forts, to *invent* cities; it became necessary to choose dukes and counts, and to settle in circles, in provinces. Cast into the center of Europe as a battlefield in every war, Germany attached itself, willy-nilly, to feudal organization, and remained barbarian in order not to perish. This is what explains the wonderful spectacle of a still young and virgin race that we see committed as though by a magic spell to a transparent civilization, the way a suddenly sealed-off liquid remains fluid in the center of an imperfect crystal.

1831. *Introduction à l'Histoire Universelle*

I have spoken in another work of the profound impersonality of the Germanic genius, and I shall return to that subject elsewhere. This characteristic is frequently disguised by the sanguinary force, which is very remarkable in German youth; as long as this intoxication of the blood lasts, there is a great deal of energy and passion here. Yet impersonality is the basic characteristic: a phenomenon admirably grasped by ancient sculpture, witness the colossal busts of Dacian captives now in the Braccio Nuovo of the Vatican, and the polychrome statues to be seen in the vestibule of our Louvre. The Dacians of the Vatican, in their enormous proportions, with their forest of unkempt hair, suggest not barbarian ferocity but rather a great brute force, that of the ox and the elephant, with something oddly vague and indeterminate about it. They see without seeming to look, rather like the statue of the Nile in the same Vatican hall, and the charming Seine by Vietti in the Lyons Museum. This indeterminacy of gaze has often struck me in the most eminent men of Germany.

1833. *Histoire de France,* I, Appendix

LA CURÉE

[*The Protestants stripped of their goods, on the revocation of the Edict of Nantes*] Which in venery is called *la curée.* And reminds us of a dreadful courtyard of Versailles, which still exists and in which was made, the evening after the hunt, the distribution of strips of flesh to the famished dogs. A tiny, very tiny courtyard, which must have been an abyss of blood, a pit of carnage. A slender interior balcony permitted the fine ladies to watch at their ease, and to savor the perfume of the place.

1860. *Histoire de France,* XIII

The Visitandines, as we knew, were awaiting the visit of the
Bridegroom, and were known as *Daughters of the Heart of
Jesus.* Yet he did not come. The worship of the heart (but
of the heart of Mary) had originated in Normandy with very
little effect. But in vinous Burgundy, where sex and blood
are rich, a Burgundian girl, a Visitandine nun of Paray, finally received the promised visit, and Jesus allowed her to
kiss the wounds of his bleeding heart.

Marie Alacoque (this was her name) had not been exhausted, depleted in early youth by the cold regime of the
convents. Cloistered late, in the full force of her life, of her
youth, the poor girl was a martyr to her sanguinary plethora. Each month, she had to be bled. And even so, she
experienced, at twenty-seven, no less of that supreme ecstasy
of celestial felicity. Beside herself, she confessed to her Ab-
bess, an able woman who took a great initiative. She dared
draw up a marriage contract between Jesus and Alacoque,
who signed with her own blood. The Mother Superior signed
boldly for Jesus. Amazingly, the wedding was performed.
Whenceforth, from month to month, the bride was visited
by the Bridegroom. (See Père Galiffet, etc.)

The Jesuits, directors of the Visitandines, did not disap-
prove. If there had been a shadow of doctrine, of mystical
spirituality, they would have been more prudent. But this
was only a fact, a material and carnal action. They said and
repeated as much: "It is the cult of the true bleeding heart,
the flesh and blood of Jesus." No need for high mysticism.
It is enough, Alacoque said, not to hate God; of himself,
Jesus will come to join his heart with yours.

The two women (Alacoque and Guyon) were both twenty-
seven years old in 1675. They transformed the Catholic world.

The spirituality of the one, and the other's materiality, so diverse in appearance, gave a new and warmer impetus to religious leadership. It was revived chiefly by the new emblem, by the dubious language which it furnished, by the ambiguity of the material and moral heart which was increasingly invoked. In twenty-five or thirty years, 428 convents of the Sacred Heart were created.

1860. *Histoire de France,* XIII, 15

THE SANGUINARY PLETHORA: MARAT'S "SENSIBILITY"

Fabre d'Églantine has evoked "Marat's sensibility." And this word has amazed those who identify sensibility with kindness, those who are not aware that an exalted sensibility can become frenzied. Women have moments of cruel sensibility. Marat, with regard to temperament, was a woman, and more, very nervous, very bloodthirsty. His physician, Monsieur Bourdier, would read his journal, and when he found it more bloodthirsty than usual, "turning red," he would proceed to bleed Marat.

1847. *Histoire de la Révolution,* II, xiv, 6

BLOOD OF STEEL: SAINT-JUST THE VIRGIN

Without his fixed, hard eyes, his heavily drawn brows, Saint-Just might have passed for a woman. Was this the virgin of Tauris? No, neither the eyes nor the skin, though white and fine-textured, suggested a sentiment of purity. This very aristocratic skin, with its singular luster and transparency, seemed too lovely, and led one to suspect its healthiness. The huge, close-knitted cravat, which he alone wore at that time, made his enemies say, perhaps without reason, that it concealed cold humors. The neck was virtually suppressed by

Saint-Just

the cravat and by the high, stiff collar; an effect all the odder in that his long waist did not lead you to expect this foreshortening of the neck. He had a very low forehead, the top of his head appearing depressed, so that the hair, without being long, almost touched the eyes. But strangest of all was his gait, of an automatic stiffness which was entirely his own. Robespierre's stiffness was nothing to this. Did it derive from a physical oddity, from his excessive pride, from a calculated dignity? —No matter. It was more intimidating than absurd. One felt that a being so inflexible in his movements must also be inflexible in his heart. Thus, when in his speech, taking up the Gironde and abandoning Louis XVI, he turned stiffly, all of a piece, to the right of the Chamber and released along with his words his whole person as well, particularly his hard and murderous stare, there was no one present who did not feel the chill of steel.

1851. *Histoire de la Révolution,* V, ix, 5

BLACK BLOOD: LOUIS XIV

The king sent the Dauphin for the erection of the statue. He himself rarely left Versailles. His blood had grown sour. The political violence of these last years, the violent diet which overexcited him, the furious counsels of Louvois, bombardments, proscriptions—everything caused an acrid humor to ferment within him. The slightest contradictions, in this state of choleric pride, become horribly painful. The king had within him an audacious contradictor—a man? no, no man would have dared—but nature dared. While he saw himself painted on the ceilings of Versailles as more than a man, a sun of youth, beauty, and vitality, this brazen nature was telling him: "You are a man." Nature permitted herself to take him in the one place where all men are humiliated. He had had tumors on his knee, and had shown patience. Nature afflicted him with another, on the anus. No remedy but a surgical one, a new and consequently serious operation which would be heard of throughout Europe and of which surgery would make a triumph, an eternal fanfare, to glorify the bold physician. He would become, like that man in Molière, *un illustre malade,* a renowned victim, a famous patient. The secret was still kept, but it could not fail to burst all bounds. What was more vexing than such waiting? Nine whole months he resisted, retreated, fearing the notoriety of this affair, thinking—not without reason—that Europe would laugh, and would take courage by such laughter.

1860. *Histoire de France,* XIII, 25

VIOLET TOMBS: SEALED BLOOD

Is it a dream? Is this a nightmare, or reality and history? This is the sad question one asks oneself looking in Bruges at the tombs of Margaret and Charles the Bold, the excessively naïve image of that system, the genealogical tree of the houses of Austria and of Burgundy:

Bella gerant alii: tu, felix Austria, nube.

All these marriages contain wars; all have been fecund in battles, in famines; these hymeneal torches have set fire to Europe. Fecund, prolific marriages; cradles crammed with mourning, rich in children and calamities; each birth deserved tears, if we remember that these countless scions imposed royal titles on distant peoples; that they required thrones; that there was not one of all these innocent nurselings who, for his milk, could not demand the blood of a million men.

Indeed, it is with reason that these graves in Bruges, of violet marble, covered with their bronze statues, trouble the mind with their at once splendid and lugubrious aspect. The trees whose copper branches embrace the stylobate, each of whose branches is an alliance, each leaf a marriage, each fruit a prince's birth, strike the ignorant eye as a laborious riddle, but, for one who knows, they are an object of dread; angels support them, charming innocent children, yet these are angels of death.

Look at Charles the Bold, ancestor of Charles V; he is the consequence of three tragedies: that of *Jean sans Peur,* of the fatal marriage which caused the death of Louis of Orléans and brought the English into France; that of *York and Lancaster,* which brought about the Wars of the Roses and killed eighty princes (but who has even bothered to count the people killed?); and finally the *tragedy of Portugal,* of Pedro the Cruel, of the bastard who established his dynasty with his dagger. Charles the Bold himself, by inheritance, marriage, and conquests, is the fatal hymen of how many states? He is their extinction, not their reconciliation, the *rapprochement* of hatred and of war. In him Flemings, Walloons, Germans combat and destroy each other. So that in a single man you see two moral battles, two absurd intersections of irreconcilable elements, which shriek at their encounter. As race and as blood, he is Burgundy, Portugal, England, he is North and South; as Prince and Sovereignty, he is five or six peoples. Or even five or six different centuries: he is barbaric Frisia, where the Germanic *Gau* of the age of Arminius still thrives; he is industrial Flanders, the Manchester of the period; he is noble and feudal Burgundy. At Dijon and at Ghent, at the chapters of the Golden Fleece, he represents a kind of Gothic Louis XIV holding the Round Table of King Arthur. He is everything, he is nothing; or, if he is, he is mad.

Thus he dies in Nancy. And thus his son-in-law survives, the great hunter Maximilian, Austro-Anglo-Portuguese. The discord of race is not a frenzy in Maximilian, but a vertigo, a futile agitation, a dizzying race to death; a goblin haunts his brain, pursues him, leads him on—leads him astray, leaving him not a moment to draw breath.

The product of these two madnesses, the son of Maximilian and grandson of Charles, Philip, will not survive. This handsome player of the Jeu du Paume wears himself out in childish diversions and dies on that field of honor. Not soon enough, though, for him to fail to marry; to the two elements of madness he inherits from his parents, he adds a third, the grim melancholia of Joanna the Mad. This queen, wretched product of the forced marriage of the Spanish peoples, of the knightly Isabella of Castile to the old and miserly *marrano* Ferdinand of Aragon, consummates in her son the union of three madnesses, three discords. This chaos of diverse elements is incarnated in Charles V.

1855. Histoire de France, VII, 13

THE ANTI-BLOOD: STONE

[*Michelet dissects women's bodies at Clamart*] In the women of the people, who had evidently practiced trades, the skull was very simple in shape, as though in a rudimentary state. These would have led me into the serious error of supposing that woman in general is, in this essential center of the organism, inferior to man. Fortunately, other skulls of women disabused me, particularly that of a woman presenting a singular pathological condition, who obliged M. Béraud to determine both her disease and her antecedents. Thus, in this case, I had what I lacked with regard to these others, the history of a life, of a destiny.

This infinitely rare singularity was a considerable calculus found in the womb. This organ, generally so corrupted nowadays but perhaps never to this degree, here revealed a

Minerality:
Francis II of Austria
"Not a man, not a mask,
but a wall of stone from
the Spielberg."
—*Histoire de la Révolution,* III, 6

very extraordinary condition. That in the very sanctuary of
life and fecundity one should find this cruel desiccation, this
frenzied atrophy, an Arabia, so to speak, a stone . . . that
the wretched woman should have been the victim of petri-
faction . . . this cast me into a sea of somber reflections.

1860. *La femme,* Introduction, 4

THE ANTI-BLOOD: NERVES

In ancient times, woman was a body. Marriage being, in
such times, merely a means of generation, one chose as one's
bride a strong creature, a red girl (red and beautiful being
synonyms in all barbarian languages). One chose her for
having a great deal of blood, and for being prepared to shed

it. One made a great deal of this. The sacrament of marriage was a baptism of blood.

In modern marriage, which is chiefly a union of souls, the soul is the essential being. The woman of modern man's dreams—delicate, ethereal—is no longer that red girl. In her the life of the nerves is everything. Her blood is merely motion and action. It is in her lively imagination, her cerebral mobility; it is in that nervous grace, that sickly *delicacy;* it is in her emotional and sometimes scintillating language; above all, it is in that profound gaze of love which sometimes inspires and enchants, sometimes troubles, and most often touches—darting straight to the heart and prompting tears.

That is what we love, what we dream of and pursue, what we desire. And now, in marriage, by a strange inconsistency, we forget all this and we seek the daughter of strong races, the country virgin who, especially in our idle and overfed cities, would abundantly possess the scarlet fountain of life.

The advent of nervous power, the bankruptcy of sanguinary force, long since under way, is moreover a phenomenon of these times. If the illustrious Dr. Broussais were to return, where would he find, in our generation (I mean, among the cultivated classes), the torrents of blood which he drew, not without success, from the veins of the men of his day? A fundamental change, for the worse? for the better? It is arguable. But what is certain is that man has been refined and made spirit. An uninterrupted explosion of great works and discoveries has marked these thirty years.

1858. *L'amour,* II

THE ACRID AND THE SOPITIVE

Who has not seen in a dusty countryside, amid the dry harvest, the green-enameled cantharides dart across the path with their fierce and jerky gait? Burning elixir of life, in which love has turned to poison! It is never with impunity that one uses it in medicine. This medieval pharmacy, dangerous to man, is not innocent, it seems, for the animals themselves. A cat which I had for a long time, quite intelligent but of an eccentric liveliness, used to hunt these cantharides. The acridity of the handsome insects seemed to attract her, as the flame the moth. It was an intoxication. But when, among the flowers, the cat had seized and chewed up her dangerous victim, the latter seemed to take its revenge. The inflammable feline nature, pricked with this spur, exploded in cries, in rages, in strange leaps. She expiated this orgy of fire by cruel pains.

Quite the contrary, another insect, the bamboo worm or malalis, if you remove the head which is a deadly poison, furnishes an exquisite cream whose gentle and sopitive effect, according to the Brazilian Indians, soothes the pangs of love. For two days and nights, a girl who has tasted this cream, sleeping beneath the flowering trees, nonetheless dreams that she is running through the depths of the virgin forests, the mysteries of the cool banks which have never seen the sun or the footsteps of human beings—nothing but the solitary flight of a great blue butterfly. But she is not alone there; love assuages its thirst on the most delicious fruits.

1857. *L'insecte,* II, 14

THE OCEAN EMPURPLED

Fine red blood, hot blood—that is the sea's triumph. With it, the ocean has animated, has armed its giants with incomparable power, far above all terrestrial creation. It has created this element; it can indeed, for you, create it over again, tinting you pink, restoring you, poor pallid flower in your weakness. The sea is overflowing with blood, superabundant. . . . In these children of the sea, blood itself is a sea which, once broached, streams and smokes, empurpling the Ocean far and wide.

Here is the revelation of the mystery. All the principles which, in you, are united, this great impersonal creature possesses, only divided. She has your bones, she has your blood, she has your vital fluid and your warmth, each element represented by one or another of her children.

And she has what you have not—excess and superabundance of power. Her breath affords something gay, creative, what might be called a physical heroism. For all her violence, the great generatrix also produces a fierce joy, a vivid and fecund alacrity, the flame of fierce love with which she herself palpitates.

1861. *La mer,* IV, 1

ANIMAL OF RED BLOOD AND OF MILK

No relation between this gentle race of mammals which have, like ourselves, red blood and milk, and the monsters of the preceding age, horrible products of the primeval slime. The whales, much more recent, found a purified water, the free seas, and the globe at peace. . . .

. . . The sea's milk, its oil, abounded; its warm, animalized fats fermented in an unheard-of power, eager for life. The sea swelled, organizing itself in these colossi, spoiled children of nature, whom she endowed with incomparable force and with what is worth still more, with fine ardent red blood. It appeared for the first time.

This is the true flower of the world. All pale-blooded creation, selfish, languishing, relatively vegetating, seems to have no heart if we compare it to the generous life which seethes in this purple, fermenting there in anger or in love. The power of the higher world, its charm, its beauty, is blood. With blood begins a new youth in nature, with blood begins a flame of desire, love, and the love of family, of race, which, extended by man, will lead to the divine crown of all life, pity.

But, with this magnificent gift, nervous sensibility is indefinitely increased. One is much more vulnerable, much more capable of taking pleasure, and also of suffering. The whale having virtually none of the hunter's senses, neither the sense of smell nor a very developed sense of hearing, everything in this creature benefits from touch. The blubber which protects it from the cold does not insure it from shocks. Its delicately organized skin, of six distinct tissues, trembles and vibrates at every touch. The tender papillae to be found there are instruments of the rarest tactility. All this is animated, vivified by a rich flow of red blood which, even taking account of the difference in size, infinitely exceeds in abundance that of terrestrial mammals. In a moment, the wounded whale floods the sea, reddens it for great distances. The blood which we possess in drops was lavished upon the whale in torrents.

The female carries her calf for nine months. Her pleasant, sweetish milk has the gentle warmth of a woman's milk. But since she must breast the waves, mammary glands placed to the fore would expose the child to every shock; they have receded somewhat lower, into a more peaceful location, at the womb from which the calf has emerged. The young are sheltered there, taking advantage of the already broken force of the waves.

A vessel shape, inherent in such a life, narrows the mother whale at the waist, and keeps her from having the rich hips of a woman, that adorable miracle of a calm, restful, and harmonious life, in which everything is dissolved into tenderness. For the whale cow, tender as she may be, everything depends on her combat with the waves. As to the rest, the organism is the same beneath this strange mask; the same form, the same sensibility. A fish above, a woman below.

1861. La mer, II, 12

FLOWER OF BLOOD

The colors do not last long. Most fade and vanish. The madrepores themselves leave only their skeletons, which one would suppose to be inorganic, and which nonetheless are merely life condensed, solidified.

Women, who have a much finer sense of this than we, have not been deceived: they have vaguely sensed that one of these trees, the coral, was a living thing. Whence a just preference. Science may have insisted that such a thing was merely stone; then, that it was merely a shrub. Women realized otherwise.

"Madame, why do you prefer to all precious stones this tree of a dubious red?" "Monsieur, it becomes my complexion. Rubies turn me pale. This, matte and duller, actually heightens the whiteness of my skin." She is correct. The two objects are related. In coral, as on her lips and on her cheeks, it is iron which causes the color (Vogel). It reddens the one, turns the other pink.

"But, madame, these glittering stones have an incomparable luster." "Yes, but this other is gentle. It has the softness of the skin, and retains its warmth. After I have worn it for two minutes, it is my own flesh, it is myself. I can no longer tell where I leave off and it begins."

"Madame, there are lovelier reds." "Doctor, leave me this one. I love it. Why? I'm not really sure . . . or if there is a reason, one as good as any other, it is because its Oriental name is the true one: flower of blood."

1861. La mer, II, 3

Athénaïs Mialaret, Michelet's second wife

HER MAJESTY THE WOMAN

What Michelet inveterately sees in Woman is Blood. When this blood is motionless, plethoric, i.e., when Woman derives strength and not weakness from it she is excluded from femininity, she is discredited. We have seen the disgust provoked by the British Pamelas, overfed virgins, or by Marie Alacoque, foundress of the Bleeding Heart of Jesus, loathsome for her sanguinary repletion. Conversely, if the blood dries up, if woman is desiccated, if, under the action of some disease, she leaves the beneficent milieu of the blood for the inferno of minerality, she loses all mythic function. In a general fashion, "that demi-male known as woman in Europe" occupies a monstrous position in Michelet's feminine repertoire because she violates the profound law of feminine blood, which is rhythm.

MICHELET TRAUMATIZED BY BLOOD *As we know, Michelet was not sparing of his declarations concerning "the crisis of love which constitutes woman, that divine rhythm which month by month measures out her time," and it is virtually certain that his unpublished Journal has no other theme. The frequency of these declarations, their excessive character, at once lyrical and meticulous—everything suggests that for Michelet the sight of feminine blood is a veritable traumatism—physical or existential—from which he derives, as always, a new organization of the universe.*

First of all, woman's regular period identifies her with a totally natural object, and thereby contrasts her entirely with man. Man, without crisis and without renewal, without turns and returns of weakness—except for the insignificant shedding of skin and emptying of the intestines—man participates only in a quotidian, not a sidereal time; his biology has no relation with the transmutation of the great elements.

Woman, on the contrary, by her monthly crisis, is identified with Nature, governed like Nature. Man stands at the gate of Nature as of a Promised Land, he can recover a cosmic function only by history, by deliberately espousing the age-old combat of Justice and of Grace. Woman is beyond history; she possesses the key of time; she is sibyl, fairy, religion. "What the Middle Ages insulted and degraded as impurity is precisely her sacred crisis; it is what constitutes her as an object of sovereignly poetic religion."

BLOOD-AS-PHILTER *Thus, it is blood which makes woman into a superhuman other, so that every shift from man to woman can only be an initiation, what Michelet calls, after Dante, transhumanation; and this initiation can only have for its philter Woman's blood. How? The feminine period, governed like the Ocean by the stars, abolishes all logical opposition between fluid and fixed. The circular flux is the very archetype of a beneficent fixity which can finally unite in itself movement and identity. Thus, Woman begins where History ends. History knows only a linear, two-phase dialectic, it is Grace or Justice, narcosis or combat, and its only movement is that of a kind of savage and jerky fecundation. "History, which we so stupidly decline in the feminine, is a rude and savage male, a sunburnt, dusty traveler; Nature is a woman." Which means that Historic Time, straight* *as a wire, but thereby fugitive, irreplaceable, is set in opposition to the Circular Time of stars, seas, and women, the time of rest and of eternity. History's mobility is imperfect because it is rectilinear ("the historical railroad track").* Woman, constitutively shunted onto a circular rhythm, is a fulfilled History, a triumphant History.*

THE REDEMPTIVE RHYTHM *Thus, feminine blood is revealed in its redemptive principle, which is rhythm. Sanguinary rhythm has as its function to superimpose a fixed time upon a moving time, it victoriously reduces two contraries, though without ever denaturing them. Which means that Woman's fixity is not established to the detriment of her weakness. Though each time it is overcome, her period disarms Woman without recourse, and it is this very destitution which makes her into a void and provokes man to vertigo and to effusion. The sanguinary crisis discovers Woman as analogous to the terrible and necessary molt of certain insects, it is an ultra-nudity, and makes Woman a being without carapace and without secret, as exposed as an ant without chitin or a chrysalis without cocoon.*

MICHELET-AS-VOYEUR *For Michelet—and how many indiscreet professions on this subject!—femininity is therefore total only at the menstrual moment. Which is to say that love's object is less to possess Woman than to discover her. "Love's sharpest goad is not so much beauty as passion." Michelet's erotics evidently takes no account of the pleasures of orgasm, whereas it attributes a considerable importance to Woman in crisis, i.e., to Woman humiliated. This is an erotics of seeing, not of pos-*

---

*For all that he owes him, Michelet retains nothing of Vico's schema of a spiral history, progressing by turns and returns.

session, and Michelet in love, Michelet fulfilled, is none other than Michelet-as-voyeur.

This frenzy to observe the secret moments of the feminine toilette is of course furnished with a moral finality, and presence-as-gaze is always naïvely given as presence-as-help. As Michelet himself said, there is a close relation between love and pity: as a matter of fact, he constantly substituted one for the other, and what he calls pity is never anything but the erotic spectacle of Woman humiliated. Whence the fantastic pages on the pleasures of the husband, admitted to the secret of his wife's periods; there is a complete transference; and it is finally woman's sanguinary moment which assumes all the erotic functions which ordinarily devolve upon beauty or virginity.

WOMAN-AS-WILD-STRAWBERRY Michelet's historical feminine repertoire is therefore constituted less by women in love than by loving women, i.e., by women sufficiently docile or sufficiently generous to give themselves to man, not as the object of a possession but as the spectacle of a crisis. Woman is therefore judged outside of any humanity; nothing monstrous in evaluating her quantity of blood, as one might evaluate the quantity of sugar in certain fruits. Away with plethoric women (Woman-as-rose, Woman-as-pineapple); what is required is the secret woman (by which we are to understand: docile to the indiscretion of her husband alone); in a word, Woman-as-wild-strawberry.

When she belongs to a country, to a class where she is supposed to place a taboo not on her sex but on her sanguinary functions, woman—the Englishwoman, for example, or the aristocrat—is excluded from the Micheletist paradise. You will find in it, on the other hand, women of the people, those of history, and Michelet's own (Rustica and Barbara), supposedly more docile or less modest. And the Negress, too, whose erotic "kindness" Michelet vaunts beyond all measure. No painful demand wearies *her obedience, "never sure of pleasing and ready to do anything to displease less." In a general fashion, the adorable woman is slender, slight, and yet accessible to suffusion, i.e., she is equally remote from sanguinary plethora and from mineral desiccation. She is conjugally compliant and without limits, not, as we know, to the male's strength, but to the husband's indiscretion. Such is the little wife of the medieval serf. Such is, above all, pale Athénaïs, though Michelet has evidently had to struggle to convince his young wife of this singular erotics.*

This is because the wifely function does not inevitably imply the ordinary conjugal duties. To be subject to man is much less to accept passively the rhythm of male attentions (Michelet never stops imploring young husbands not to do violence to their wives) than to yield to this sacred indiscretion, whose nature we know. Some have imagined Athénaïs's drama as that of a frigid, cerebral, ambitious young woman surrendered by marriage to a greedy old man. The demand was perhaps of another order, and the resistance as well. There is no other explanation for the mystery of a Journal intime *hidden so long because it is probably still shocking—more to manners than to morals. The taboos of education are more severe than those of sex.*

MAN-AS-CHAMBERMAID   *This transposition of the art of loving compels a special kind of Don Juanism. It is not a question of being physically pleasing to women, but of gaining their confidence to the point where they consent to reveal the secret of their periods. The Micheletist technique is therefore not one of conquest but of persuasion. It is no use for the man to be young; since what is involved is gaining access to a secret (in the eyes of the world, the most repulsive; in the eyes of Michelet, the most poetic), and not to an attraction, the husband should be an older man, uniting in his own person all the situations which justify unreserved abandon: like Michelet at the time of* his second marriage, he will be in his fifties and a professor, at once a father and a lay priest. Above all, he is a Don Juan-confessor. And since the erotic act itself is reduced to the most difficult of confidences, it matters little whether or not a woman is apt at lovemaking: only her period is her attraction. Woman can therefore be frigid (as young Athénaïs was), marriage is not spoiled because of that; man finds his sufficient harmony not in woman possessed but in the spectacle violated.

It follows that the husband is no longer, strictly speaking, male, genitor, and master; he is essentially a spectator. His functions can therefore, without false modesty, be those of all the persons who have some right to approach the young wife in her most intimate circumstances. In order to fulfill his duty, the husband must occupy, in relation to his wife, all the sites of a sort of peripheral relationship: he must be at once bridegroom, lover, mother, page, chambermaid, physician. The important thing is to try to exhaust all the situations of feminine companionship. Thinking of Woman, Michelet assigns himself as constant rival not the man, the lover, but above all the Confessor, of either sex, for it is this function which renders the Confessor dangerous. This Confessor-as-rival can be the Priest, of course, but also the Chambermaid, the Julie who unduly possesses, at her mistress's side, the longed-for power of contemplating and attending her during her periods: a privilege of a sacred order which ought to be the husband's alone, since as a matter of fact it constitutes the erotic moment par excellence.

MICHELET'S LESBIANISM *For Michelet, relations between man and woman are therefore not at all based on the difference between the sexes; male and female are moral figures intended to judge conventionally certain historical states or phenomena: History is male, Syria is female. But in erotic terms, there is only a spectator and his spectacle; Michelet himself is no longer either man or woman, he is nothing but Gaze; his approach to woman compels him to have no specifically virile characteristic. On the contrary: since it is generally the male who is kept away, by a kind of genetic taboo, from Woman's sanguinary crisis, Michelet seeks to strip the genitor away from himself; and since this crisis is made a spectacle exclusively for other women, for companions, mothers, sisters, nurses, and servants, Michelet turns himself into a woman, mother, nurse, the bride's companion. In order to force his way into the gynaeceum more surely, not as a ravisher but as a spectator, the old lion puts on a skirt, attaches himself amorously to Woman by a veritable lesbianism, and finally conceives of marriage only as a kind of sororal couple.*

The ideal movement of love is not, for Michelet, penetration but juxtaposition, for it is not sex but seeing which gives its measure. Just as, when regarding the fish as gelatinized water, Michelet constituted the universe as a deliciously smooth object, so to protect Woman, to cover her, to envelop her, to "follow" her entire surface, is to do away with any discontinuity of substance. The ideal figure of the lover is ultimately the garment: no more difference between algae and fish than between skin and the silk which covers it. When Michelet amorously describes the tunic coiled around woman, there is no doubt that he longs to be that garment and sees himself as such, a secret pursued, clung to, absorbed in extent and not in depth.

SACRAL ROYALTY OF WOMAN *Which constitutes man as Woman's parasite. Woman is Queen, man her slave. This is no metaphor: we are concerned with a royalty of a sacral order: Woman is an absolute Other.*

First of all, she does not have the same body as man: she differs from him by her cardinal elements: her blood, with its rhythm; her breath, moved by the ribs, presenting the gentle undulation of her breasts, i.e., transparency of the emotions; her nourishment, light, almost insubstantial, ambrosian; her language finally, superior to that of bird and man alike, an entirely magical language, a language of the gods. And then, a body constituted of another flesh, more angelic than human, woman establishes for each object the very measure of ideality. Consider her hair, for example; do not compare it to silk, but say rather that the finest fiber seeks the perfection of a woman's hair. Woman constitutes a cosmic element, an ultra-planetary metal, a kind of superlative state of matter, at once original (in the beginning was the Woman) and terminal (the future City will be matriarchal).

As a matter of fact, Woman is an element at once contiguous and exterior to humanity, a kind of complete environment for man; a milieu, in fact. "It is true of her as of heaven for earth, it is above and beneath, all round. We are born within her. We live upon her. We are enveloped by her. We breathe her, she is the atmosphere, the element of our heart." Being element and not individual, woman is superior by nature to any civil law: she is unpunishable. We are not thereby to understand that she is necessarily innocent. Woman is not infantile; she can be guilty, even responsible; but her humanity ceases at the moment of repression, like that of a disguised god who becomes a god again if threatened with death.

WOMAN HUMILIATED *We are to note that this monarchy of woman must be constantly returned to its basis, which is the sanguinary period, i.e., Woman weakened, subjugated, humiliated. It is in the moment of her greatest weakness that, manifesting her otherness, she affirms her magical power. Man must therefore not cease to spy upon the humiliated Woman, for it is at the very moment when he sees her empty, available, subject to the lunar rhythm, that she can be the medium for him, con-*

ductrix of the beneficent cycle of Nature. Hence, you will find in Micheletist history a good number of women humiliated, always by some indiscreet gaze (Jeanne d'Arc and the soldiers, Queen Anne and Sarah Marlborough, Woman bathing in the sea), and it is in these pitilessly noted episodes that Michelet finds the excessive lyricism of a bard whose strophe periodically reestablishes a monarchy.

WOMAN IS RELIGION *A necessary tyranny, for it alone saves man from History by replacing him within a circular time, at once in movement and fixed. Let man—deprived, alas, of any biological rhythm—hand himself over to Woman; let him espouse, by a scrupulous attention, the beneficent returns of the sanguinary period: he will do away with the degradations of linear time in himself, he will live several lives, in the fashion of the great Magi. Woman is therefore an ultimate medication, she halts time and, better still, makes it begin again. Woman legitimately bears superhuman names; she is Fairy, Sibyl, Sorceress; though her man accedes to a superior knowledge, she is religion, initiation. Having become the very figure of nature by the regular return of exaltation, she constitutes for man an omega of wisdom. Hence, only old men can approach Woman; their belated loves have something unfathomable—mysterious acts of seeing rather than passions.*

"Gentle mediator between Nature and man," Woman is a key, she opens. Consider Rousseau, ordinarily tense, grim, mute; a single power released him, restored him to language, genius, sociability: Women; they forced him open, made him give birth. Consider again the Middle Ages, a sealed epoch if ever there was one. It is Woman, under the name of Witch, who sustained the*

---

*Any historical study of Michelet should pay the closest attention to the Gnostic halo around his thought. Cf. Nerval, Ballanche, Balzac, Comte, and Renan (*L'Abesse de Jouarre*).

great current of the beneficent sciences of nature. The history of
her diseases is the history of humanity itself. The sixteenth century was a Renaissance to the degree that Paracelsus and Fal-
lopius discovered the Fons Viventium, the profound otherness of
Woman, subject to the effect of a single organ, the womb, and
of a single function, the sacred flux. But this was still only a
preparatory phase. The nineteenth century, a fatal century in
which History ceases, is saved by the great revolution of embryogeny and ovology, so that here again it is Woman who snatches
up the torch of failing History. The Revolution ended historic
time for good: natural time begins: Woman, discovered in the
mystery of her flux,* advenes and will reign.

MATRIA   The demoniac City, then, is the city of men only
(the Templars, for example). The ideal City can only be matriarchal. This means that it will be virtually insectiform, since
it is in the order of wasps, of bees, and of ants that females form
the most indisputable of aristocracies.

The matriarchal City, moreover, has its historical prefigura-
tions: Sparta is the world-as-wasp, Athens the world-as-bee.
Converse proof of this similitude: the ant is "powerfully republican." But let there be no mistake: Michelet does not choose
Matria by reason of its fecundating power. Doubtless, fecundity,
the strictly maternal aptitude, is a beneficent value; it can justify
a certain sympathy. But it is not at all the cardinal virtue of the
insect world. The true female, the female who gives birth and
perpetuates, is discredited by her insipid and larval whiteness.
Above the soft, weak genetrix doomed to a vegetative parturi-
tion, the natural city possesses laborious virgins "who dedicate
themselves entirely to an adoptive maternity." These ants, "aunts

* Michelet cites in this regard the works of Geoffroy and Serres on embryogeny,
of Bauer on ovology, and, generally, the popularizing action of the Faculty of
Sciences and of the Collège de France from 1840 to 1850.

and sisters," constitute an ideal order of rulers. We here rediscover the sororal theme: it is not the fecund woman who matters
to Michelet (does not gestation deprive her of her essential con-
stitution, which is the sanguinary rhythm?); it is Woman-as-
Sister, woman by the regular movements of her blood, and sister
by her power of confiding such "secrets of nature." No doubt in
this ideal society of insects, Michelet regards himself much less
as a drone than a sister himself, deliciously divided between the
laborious function of the aunt-virgins and their femininity revealed and seen at will.

LANGUAGE-AS-NURSE   All this feminine mythology evidently involves a special language. By a cruel mockery, Michelet
is unable to speak of Woman save in the most artificial tonality
of all, that of the Novel (maleficent theme in Micheletist history). Consider the great feminine episodes in his work: Jeanne
d'Arc, the Witch, Madame Legros (who saved Jean-Henri La-
tude), Katya the Russian serf, the black Virgin of the Song of
Songs; they are heroines of novels, and novels at once salacious
and silly: no one is unaware of their little physical humiliations,
those "things of nature" which rendered them adorable in Michelet's memory; but Michelet continues to call these women, de-
nuded more audaciously than by any libertine author, jeunes
demoiselles, "young ladies," and to brandish in their regard all
the insipid graces of petit-bourgeois language. Here too, ultimately, there is no reason to be surprised: the stupefying speech
of mères de famille was an additional pleasure because it constituted Michelet as the official owner of femininity. In order to
make himself more certainly a matron, the authorized guardian
of Woman's physical secrets, the masterly historian, the enormous vorator of all human history, voluptuously entrusts himself
to language-as-nurse.

Michelet
Engraving by Boilvin

And it is not yet over. The fear must remain undiminished. There she is in her lace, pale, and lovely with a touching charm. Ah, if you knew, in truth, the terrible reality such beauty conceals!

One must face up to everything, O man. Such impressions are salutary. You must know well the great master of suffering, Love. . . .

"No, have mercy," you will say. "Leave us our poetry, what is horrible is not poetic. What would she herself become if we were to show her the shocking image of her lacerated entrails?"

Let us spare her such a sight, but you, you must endure it, and it will do you good.

Nothing subdues the senses more. Whoever has not been hardened, made blasé by such mournful spectacles, is scarcely his own master, upon seeing the exact depiction of the womb after it has given birth. A tremulous pain sets in and sends chills up the spine. . . . The prodigious irritation of the organ, the murky stream which exudes so cruelly from the devastated furrow, oh! what horror! . . . One turns away. . . .

This was my impression when this truly terrible object was presented to me for the first time in the excellent plates of Bourgery's book. An incomparable drawing from the Atlas of Coste and Gerbe also shows the same organ in a less alarming aspect, though one which stirs us to tears. It is shown at the moment when, by its infinite network of red fibers which seem to be so many silks, so many purple hairs, the womb weeps tears of blood.

1858. *L'amour,* IV

WOMAN-AS-WILD-STRAWBERRY

One day when I was renewing acquaintance, after twenty years' absence, with a Frenchman living abroad who had married there, I asked him, smiling, if he had not married some splendid British rose, or a lovely German blonde. He answered seriously, though not without a certain vivacity: "Yes, monsieur, they are very lovely, more so than our own. I compare them to those splendid fruits which gardeners train to reach the greatest possible development: the magnificent pine strawberries. Their flavor is not inferior, and it fills the mouth; one regrets only the scent. I have preferred a Frenchwoman, indeed one from the Midi, for she is the wild strawberry."

1859. *La femme,* II, 2

THE NEGRESS

Precisely where she remains a Negress and cannot refine her features, the black woman's body is splendid. She has a charm of suave youth unknown to the Greek beauty created by gymnastics and always somewhat masculinized. She might scorn not only the odious Hermaphrodite but also the muscular beauty of the Crouching Venus (*vide* the Jardin des Tuileries). The black woman is much more a woman than the proud Greek citizen-maids; she is essentially young, in blood, heart, and body, gentle with a childish humility, never sure of pleasing and ready to do anything to displease less. No painful demand wearies her obedience. Anxious about her countenance, she is not at all reassured by its fulfilled contours of touching softness and elastic freshness. She prostrates at your feet what you were about to worship. She trembles and asks for mercy; she is so grateful for the pleasures she gives! . . . She loves and all her love has passed into her warm embrace.

1859. La femme, II, 1

"THE CHARMING MYSTERY OF YOUR LIFE"

January 3, 1849, midnight

My heart is so sick, trembling so, stirred so, so helpless to calm its palpitations, that I turn back to writing again. Ah! beloved, what will become of me, being to this degree in your hands? Ah, let them be good to me, and gentle, otherwise *I die.*

I have made great efforts to make you forget, in speaking of one thing and another, the unsuitable, audacious letter I had written. So long as I was with you, I kept my countenance. Once I had left you, I felt quite ill, my teeth clenched, my heart contracted, or pounding within my breast. I would have come to see you tomorrow, but afterwards, quite probably, I would have had to take to my bed. At this very moment, I am still trembling with fever. I am not accusing you, my friend, ah! you were entitled to make quite different reproaches. The one you did make, yes, it was deserved. The violent love I feel for your body, as for your soul, makes me subtle, perhaps even penetrating, but finally, I confess, greedy for the charming mystery of your life, and more than

I am entitled to reveal, at the very inception of this affection.

Believe me as you like, but what produces this ardent longing for your body is to see it joined to that noble mind, to that lovely, generous, heroic heart of yours. Your body fascinates me all the more, in that I am so amazed that you should have a body at all, you who, to read you, to hear you speak, seem to be pure spirit.

I had never felt this so intensely as yesterday, after my strange letter. You gave me occasion to admire you, to adore you, for your proud and noble decision, sacrificing to me your habits, your friendships, perhaps your family, bestowing upon me all the religious sentiments of your early years. Ah! I feel transfixed with respect and with religion for you.

May I become worthy of such a sacrifice! And it is perhaps the excess of my worship of you extended to your entire person which has made me so bold as to touch upon these difficult subjects. In you, everything seems adorable and holy. I kiss your hand, if you will permit me.

J.M.

Unpublished letters to Mlle Mialaret

MAN-AS-CHAMBERMAID

. . . And if there must be a chambermaid for other delicate attentions, I shall offer you one who eagerly aspires to the position, who has a hundred times more enthusiasm than Mademoiselle Julie, than Mademoiselle Lisette and all the celebrated examples of the type, and one who furthermore is not sly, who will never gossip about you to the neighbors, who will not grimace behind your back when you are speaking, etc. —But where is this treasure to be found? I shall hire her, she is what I need. . . . —Where is she? At your side.

Here is your subject, O queen, who petitions to enter into your service; he believes he has been promoted if you raise him to the dignity of *valet de chambre,* to the feudal position of Chamberlain, Chief Domestic, Grand Master of your house, or indeed, Physician-in-ordinary (at least with regard to hygiene), for his zeal knows no limits. All these court duties he will accomplish *gratis,* and in addition, along with the functions of men, he will execute those of women, proud and honored, madame, if Your Majesty will accept his very humble services.

1858. *L'amour,* II, 7

A physician who happens to be an excellent husband once told me: "In your book, the best part is what has provoked so much laughter, the quasi-maternal attentions of love, the voluntary servitudes which do away with the chambermaid. This tiresome, dangerous interloper is a wall between spouses which renders their relations fortuitous. One is on visiting terms with one's own wife, as though with a kept mistress. The advantage of marriage is that one has all the time in the world; hence the rare favorable moments when a woman, since all are a little slow, can be brought to feel real emotion. Affection, gratitude, do a great deal for her. Women are the more easily stirred by the man who has been able to manage the little mysteries and who tends them with affection in their weaknesses of nature. If you would understand woman, remember that in natural history the mating season constitutes the weakness, the faltering of all creatures. Terrible in the lower species, it yields them up defenseless to their enemies. Man, in whom fortunately it is not violent, constantly sheds his skin, even the internal epidermis. In his daily intestinal discharge, he gives a great deal of himself and feels weak. Woman loses much more, having in addition the vaginal flux of each month. She has what all creatures have in their seasons, the need to hide, but also to seek support. She is the Mélusine of the fairy tale: a lovely fairy who was often, below the waist, a pretty snake, hiding herself away in order to molt. Happy the man who can reassure Mélusine, give her confidence, and act as her nurse! And who would do it better? It is actually a profanation to expose this dear and timid person (in such an innocent matter) to the sly tricks of an indiscreet creature who might expose her to laughter. Such an excess of intimacy must devolve upon the only one for whom it is a felicity and a favor. This favor costs her dear at first, but gradually she will find it very sweet, and be unable to do without it. Nature loves habit, and is powerfully assisted by the absolute liberties of childhood. These are happy moments, of grace and favorable attendance, of ready sympathy, in which the beloved *confidant* gains the ascendancy of a harmless magnetism. The charming humility (in which she feels so readily that she is queen) has no defense and yields entirely. A profound oblivion, an abandon without reservation. Love, as in a kind of dream, occasionally encounters here the rare opportunity of utter happiness, the salutary crisis (so profound among women) in which life bestows itself altogether in order to renew itself forthwith and be restored to youth, embellished as nature would have it."

1859. *La femme,* Notes

MARRIAGE OF SKIN AND SILK

. . . The great and the profound effects are not those of dressed silk. Silk left in its natural state and not even dyed is in a more intimate relation with woman and with beauty. Amber and pearls, slightly less yellow, with old-fashioned lace, are the only objects that silk enjoys as its companions.

Noble embellishment, never brash, which lends a gentle charm to the vivacities of youth, and gives to pallid beauty its most warming effect.

Here there is a true mystery which enchants us. Color or sheen? Cotton has a shimmer of its own and, when properly finished, often assumes a delightful coolness. Silk is not strictly shiny, but rather luminous, of a gentle electric light, quite naturally in accord with woman's electricity. A living tissue, it gratefully embraces the living body.

Ladies of the Orient, before they adopted the stupid fashions of the West, had only two garments, for outer wear the true cashmere (so fine that the thickest shawl could pass through a ring) and, underneath, a lovely tunic of pale silk, strewn with the reflections of magnetic amber.

These two garments were less garments than friends, gentle slaves, supple and charming flatterers: warm, caressing cashmere, yielding to everything, coiling of its own accord, after the bath, around the shivering bather; the silk tunic, on the other hand, light, airy, not too diaphanous: its pallor wed it perfectly to the matte surface of human skin: one might have said that it took its color from its constant intimacy with and its tender habitude of the skin. Inferior to skin, no doubt, yet it seemed something of a sister to it, or rather it ended by becoming part of the human person, dissolving into it, in a sense, the way a dream melts into all of existence and cannot be separated from it ever again.

1857. *L'insecte,* II, 13

WOMAN'S OTHERNESS

She does nothing as we do. She thinks, speaks, acts differently. Her tastes differ from our tastes. Her blood has not the same rate as ours, at moments it rushes, like a storm shower. She does not breathe as we do. Anticipating pregnancy and the future ascent of the lower organs, nature has caused her to breathe mainly by the four upper ribs. From this necessity results woman's greatest beauty, the gentle undulation of the breast, which expresses all her sentiments in a mute eloquence.

She does not eat as we do, or as much, or the same dishes. Why? Chiefly because she does not digest as we do. Her digestion is troubled at every moment by one thing: she loves, from the very depth of her bowels. The deep cup of love (which we call the pelvis) is a sea of variable emotions which counter the regularity of the nutritive functions.

These internal differences are produced externally by yet another, more striking one: woman has a language of her own. Insects and fish remain mute. The bird sings. It seeks to articulate. Man has a distinct language, an exact and luminous speech, the clarity of the word. But woman, above man's word and the song of the bird, has an entirely magical language with which she interrupts that word or that song: the sigh, her impassioned breath.

Incalculable power. No sooner is it felt than our heart is stirred. Her breast rises, sinks, rises again: she cannot speak, and we are convinced in advance, won over to all she wishes. What argument of a man's will act so powerfully as a woman's silence?

1858. *L'amour,* I, 1

A WOMAN'S HAIR

The ideal of the human arts in sewing and weaving, I was once told by a southerner (a manufacturer, but inspired), the ideal we pursue, is a fine hair from a woman's head. Oh, we know that the softest wools, the finest cottons are far from achieving it—we know the enormous distance that separates and will always separate all our progress from such a hair! We lag far behind, and gaze with envy upon that supreme perfection which every day nature creates as if in play.

That delicate, strong, resistant hair, vibrating with a light sonority which runs from ear to heart, and even so is soft, warm, luminous, and electric . . . this is the flower of the human flower.

1857. *L'insecte,* II, 13

IN THE BEGINNING WAS THE WOMAN

Sprenger said (before 1500): "One must speak of the *heresy of witches,* and not of wizards; the latter are insignificant." And another voice, under Louis XIII: "For every wizard, ten thousand witches."

"Nature makes them witches." It is the genius proper to Woman and her temperament. She is born a fairy. By the regular return of exaltation, she is born a sibyl. By love, she is a sorceress. By her delicacy, her (often whimsical and beneficent) cunning, she is a witch and determines fate, or at least lulls and deceives all pains, all disease.

Every primitive people has the same beginnings; we see this in the *Voyages.* The man hunts and fights. The woman contrives, imagines; she gives birth to dreams and gods. She is a *seeress* on certain days; she has the infinite wings of desire and of dreams. The better to calculate the weather, she observes the sky. But the earth has her heart no less. Eyes lowered upon the amorous flowers, young and herself a flower, she makes a personal acquaintance with them. A woman, she asks them to heal those she loves.

Simple and touching inception of religions and sciences! Later, all will be divided; we shall see the origins of the specialist—juggler, astrologist, or prophet, necromancer, priest, physician. But, in the beginning, Woman is all.

A powerful and living religion, like Greek paganism, begins with the sibyl and ends with the witch. The sibyl, a lovely virgin in broad daylight, cradled it, gave it its enchantment, its aureole. Later on, fallen, sick, in the shadows of the Middle Ages, on the moorlands and in the woods, it was hidden by the witch; her intrepid pity nursed it, kept it alive. Thus, for the religions, Woman is a mother, a tender guardian, and a loyal nurse. The gods are like men; they are born and they die on her breast.

1862. La sorcière, Introduction

WOMEN ARE NOT PUNISHABLE

Against women there is no serious means of repression. Simple imprisonment is already a difficulty: *"Quis custodiet ipsos custodes?"* They corrupt everything, break everything; no closure is powerful enough. But to lead them to the scaffold, great God! A government guilty of such a stupidity guillotines itself. Nature, which above all laws sets love and the perpetuation of the species, has thereby placed in women this mystery (absurd at first glance): *they are indeed responsible yet they are not punishable.* In all the Revolution, I find them violent, conspiring, quite often guiltier than the men. But once one strikes them, one strikes oneself. Who punishes them punishes himself. Whatever they have done, under whatever guise they appear, they overturn justice, destroying all notion of it, causing it to be cursed and denied.

1853. Histoire de la Révolution, VII, 2

WOMAN HUMILIATED: THE FIRST SEA BATHING

Whoever has seen emerging from the water the poor creature taking one of her first baths in the sea, who sees her pale, timorous, haggard, shivering, realizes the harshness of such an attempt, and all that is dangerous in it for certain constitutions. You may be certain that no one will face so painful an ordeal, if for it there can be substituted, at home and without danger, a gentle and prudent form of hydro-therapy.

Add that this impression, as if it were not strong enough, is aggravated for the nervous woman by the presence of the crowd. It is a cruel exhibition before a critical world, before rivals delighted to find her ugly for once, before frivolous, stupidly mocking and pitiless men who observe, binoculars in hand, the pathetic bathing accidents of a wretched, hu-miliated woman.

To endure all this, the sick woman must have faith, a deep faith in the sea—she must believe that no other remedy will do, she must desire at all costs to *assimilate* the virtues of these waters.

. . .

Moreover, one must indulge in this violent emotion of cold bathing only when prepared by the habit of warm bathing which facilitates absorption. Our skin, which throughout consists of tiny mouths, and which in its way absorbs and digests even as the stomach does, needs to ac-custom itself to this powerful nourishment, to drink the *mu-cus* of the sea, that salty milk which is its life, out of which it makes and remakes all beings. In a gradual series of warm, lukewarm, and almost-cold baths, the skin will by degrees become accustomed and will inure itself to such a need: it will develop a thirst for it, and drink ever more deeply.

For the harsh ceremony of the first cold baths, one must at least escape the odious stare of crowds. Let this event occur in a safe place, without any but indispensable wit-nesses, some devoted person* who will offer assistance if

*This can only be Michelet himself, at once Sister, Nurse, and Woolens.

need be, who will keep watch, protect, and offer a rubdown, at the difficult moment of emergence, with very warm woolens, who will provide a light cordial of some warm drink, in which a few drops of some powerful elixir has been mixed.

"But," it will be objected, "the danger is less in the general view. We are far from Bernardin de Saint-Pierre's Virginie, who in extreme peril preferred to drown rather than be immersed in the sea." Wrong. We are more nervous than we ever were. And the impression of which I am speaking is so intense and so distressing, for certain persons at least, that it can involve mortal effects—aneurysm, apoplexy.

1861. *La mer,* IV, 5

ROUSSEAU UNBOUND BY WOMEN

The true Rousseau is born of women, born of Madame de Warens. He says as much himself, quite clearly. Before her, he did not speak, was tongue-tied and mute. Out of her presence, he had no ease of language, no facility. In her presence, perfect freedom, facility of elocution, abundant and warm speech.

Separated from her, and cast away upon the harsh cobbles of Paris, he tricked himself out as a Roman, as a citizen, as a savage. He followed Mably, Morelly, with the talent, the harsh strength it was so easy for him to assume. And with that, *bound.* He reconquered his nature, was once again *unbound,* only by Madame d'Houdetot. The grimace vanished, as did Cato and the Genevan. And in true passion reappeared the Savoyard.

1867. *Histoire de France,* XVII, 4

The book, taken separately, remains admirable for its quite Syrian local beauty, anything but edifying, seared with physical love, filled with a morbid inspiration, with a certain fever, a kind of autumnal breeze, deadly and delicious.

The story is not obscure, as has been claimed. In truth, it is all too clear. It is spring, the moment when in Syria (in Greece and elsewhere, too) a festival was held to broach and taste the wines of the last harvest. It is the moment when Adonis's red blood flowed at Byblos with the sands of the stream, a stream of love itself, of frenzied pleasure, of tears. A handsome young man (son of an emir, I imagine), very young, for he is "of ivory" *(eburneus)*, pale, delicate, has come to the cellars which are hollowed out of the mountain near the city, in order to broach and taste the wine. On his way, he sees a lovely brown maid, richly gilded by the Oriental sun, who tends her vines nearby. He invites her to come, to enter, to taste. She is utterly ignorant. This youth has a voice so gentle that he seems to her a girl, a young sister. She obeys, follows him, and I do not know whether he makes her drink, but she emerges trembling. She says: "Again, and kiss me with a kiss of thy mouth! . . . To touch thee is sweeter than the wine thou hast made me drink . . . what sweet-smelling odor comes from thee? I shall follow thee by thy perfume."

The innocent child's admiration is the white breast of the feminine youth *(ubera)*, "ivory overlaid with sapphire" *(Venter ejus eburneus, distinctus saphiris,* V, 14). She compares herself and blushes, making excuses for not being white. "I am black, because the sun hath looked upon me: my mother's children were angry with me, they made me the keeper of the vineyards; but my own vineyard have I not kept . . ."

I can still see her delicate, mournful smile. She makes no

complaint. But I can guess: her little heart is uneasy. If her brothers are her masters, it is because she is an orphan. Will she not be abused? I fear she will. As does she. She appears to feel that now it is he who must protect her. She presses against him, and would not leave him. "Tell me, thou whom my soul loveth, where thou feedest, where thou makest thy flock to rest at noon?" (In her simplicity, she supposes he keeps his flocks himself.) And when he says nothing, she adds with a tender threat to make him jealous: "For why should I be as one that turneth aside by the flocks of thy companions?" But she can get nothing out of him. He covers her with compliments, with caresses, and promises her splendid jewels.

She is a poor girl. He is rich. Obviously, he is afraid she will attach herself to him in this way. Is he old enough to marry? Would he not prefer to forget? We cannot say.

It is a common enough story. But not what follows. A charming and terrible power is revealed in this girl. She is carried away, transformed by love and by passion. The seven Spirits are in her, as in Sarah and in the Magdalene who out of a word made a world. This girl's power is to have none, to follow the storm wildly, blindly, to keep nothing back, to say: "I die of love," to say . . . what a woman never says. At which point the little poem, like the winged rout of demons, rushes on, sweeping all before it.

The beloved comes, returning in spite of himself. . . . In vain he escapes, evades. There is even one moment, the wretch, when he laughs at the poor little creature, boasts of his conquest among his friends. Yet, for all that, he is vanquished. The wonder is that actually, in seven nights, she has grown up quite supernaturally. She is noble and proud, she is a queen; he is amazed by her; he is almost frightened by her, so imposing is she, and so beautiful. In short, she is the lady of his house.

Everyone knows this song by heart, the splendid scene where she is lying sick, oh! so sick, and fainting, tended by her friends—the terrible and stormy night when, scented and prepared, she awaits him, hears him, believes she feels him coming, trembles. Misery! he has gone! She runs through the dark town, meets soldiers, is beaten, hurt. He is kindhearted, is touched, returns, brings jewels, sandals, and fine garments. Here he is dazed by her, he no longer laughs, he prostrates himself before her.

This moment decides everything. "Let us go forth into the field [and this last chapter clearly shows that she will live with him]; let us lodge in the villages. Let us get up early to the vineyards; let us see if the vine flourish, whether the tender grape appear. There will I give thee my loves . . . and at our gates are all manner of pleasant fruits, new and old, which I have laid up for thee, O my beloved." (*Dabo tibi ubera.*)

Evening has come. They reach the solitary countryside. She says the mandrakes "give a smell" (which makes women fruitful). A tender insinuation which, it appears, is not lost on him. The next morning, upon seeing her quite different, and perhaps already a mother, as though transfigured by some Oriental grace, he exclaims proudly, with all the rhetoric of the East: "Who is this that cometh up from the wilderness, leaning upon her beloved?"

All this is nature, is the noonday blood, is this particular climate of love. Only, I confess, we cannot read it without bewilderment. I prefer the pure love of Rama and Sita, the scene where the holy mountain, as virginal as its snows, rains down its flowers upon them. Here there are too many perfumes, harsh and strong herbs, and spiced wines. I do not know if the Shulamite, like Esther, has spent "six months with oil of myrrh and six months with sweet odors," but the scented oil which swims in the cup of love makes one hesitate to drink from it. From versicle to versicle, there is myrrh and more myrrh, all the perfumes of the embalmers. Enough for at least three dead men: spikenard, the black Indian root (of valerian, catnip), which has so powerful an effect on the nerves; cinnamon, and who knows how many aromatics of all kinds, from the insipid scent of the lily to the bitter and scorching aloe, which shoots up its flower every ten years . . .

1864. *La bible de l'humanité,* II, 6

The peoples of the twilight: Egypt

In 1825, Michelet buys a reproduction of Dürer's *Melancholy*
for his study. In it he sees "all of Faust's thought"

THE ULTRA-SEX

Fated to approach Woman as a confidant and not as a ravisher, Michelet could only be man and woman both. He does not fail to present a double sex as the ideal one, and androgynous man as the complete one. For Michelet, the two sexes of the mind are nothing but the male force of the idea and the female milieu of instinct. All creation will therefore be divided into two ways of knowledge: that of the mind and that of the heart. For example, there will be male religions (Roman law) and female religions (Christianity), male sciences (history) and female sciences (natural history). Of course, the divorce of the two sexes is disastrous: the nineteenth century, for instance, a dead century had it not discovered Woman, is imperfect insofar as it sets instinct in opposition to reflection.

HEART AND REASON *This old romantic pair of heart and reason, of spontaneity and reflection, of religion and philosophy, is found in Vico (where the* verum, *a Cartesian truth of an intellectual nature, is set in opposition to the* certum, *an emotional truth, collective by definition), where Michelet may have got it. Its immediate heredity is purely Gnostic: knowledge can discover its object only by means of feeling (Lessing, Herder, the illuminists, Ballanche, the Saint-Simonians). This Gnostic doc-*

trine was chiefly contrasted with the encyclopedist philosophy, and Michelet was caught in a contradiction: on the one hand, unreservedly to praise the eighteenth century; on the other, to admit that its excessively "cerebral" great men were incomplete. Michelet has a few rather embarrassed sentences on the matter. But his embarrassment does not last because the eighteenth century is not judged outside the Revolution: now, if the masters of the Revolution—the philosophes—*had only one sex of the mind, the men of the Revolution themselves were double, complete, male and female at the same time, to the degree where the Revolution is no longer History (i.e., a system of causes and influences) but the People, i.e., an absolute.*

THE ADVENT OF COFFEE *As a matter of fact, nothing superior is possible without the union of these two sexes, and yet one must prevail over the other. Now, paradoxically, the main role is not assigned to the fecundating (i.e., male) order. To the degree that the idea is identified with an electrical or even mechanical phenomenon, it joins the maleficent substance of dry heat, of the fire which flames without smoldering. Here we must recall Michelet's horror of the galvanic movements of matter. The idea (by which we are to understand the purely intellectual invention), hypostasis of the spark, is always presented as an anti-erotic power: consider what can artificially produce it: coffee, for instance. Coffee is an ambiguous substance: no doubt it participates in the Revolutionary glory, for its advent in the eighteenth century has brought with it critical lucidity, the black spark which destroys the slumbrous old order. And yet coffee, "the alibi of sex," is itself merely a part of that infernal trilogy (the dozing off of love) of which tobacco and alcohol are the other two members.*

THE LOVES OF THE ALOE *Coffee, idea, spark—despite the respect due to Voltaire and Diderot—three mimicries of false fecundation. This is the same discredit that Michelet evidently attaches to the orgasm, excluded from his erotic heaven insofar as it is alien to the ceremonial of devotion with which man is to surround Woman. Caricature of union, the orgasm is merely solitude and sadness. So at least Michelet describes it in the loves of the Aloe, that harsh African flower.*

THE ANDROGYNOUS HERO *Hence the idea (critical reflection) has only a tiny share in the conjunction of the sexes of the mind. It is the incubating element, the female power, which leads the nuptials. In other words, the order of operations is inverted: it is not reflection which corrects instinct, it is the heart, it is intuition which gives the idea its complete form. To the dry and sterile spark of intelligence (of the male orgasm), we must set in opposition the homogeneous warmth of incubation (of the female milieu). Superlative beings, countries, and elements will always be predominantly female, fruitful only insofar as they possess the "gift of incubation," the female power which transforms the idea into sentiment.*

The Micheletist heroes are therefore, by definition, androgynous beings,* hatching intellectual power beneath a kind of supernatural intuition, borrowed from Woman. Consider Jeanne d'Arc. It is not her pure femininity which makes her a heroine; it is because, woman that she is, she knows both sexes of the mind, "common sense in exaltation." † The same combination recurs in the other Micheletist heroes, Rabelais, Luther, Hoche, Kosciuszko. Without Woman, no masculine genius; but without

* Androgyny is never anything but a false mixture: no one can avoid seeing in it a female preponderance.

† "The Maid's originality, what constituted her success, was not so much her valor as her visions: it was her common sense." —*Histoire de France*, V, 3

The Hero-as-Child: Hoche

Danton-as-Bull

a little of the male spark, no heroine. The definition of genius is to be man and woman, a state that we can call simplicity, i.e., the combination of knowledge and ignorance which comes after knowledge, that second ignorance Pascal speaks of.

Michelet does not fail to attribute this terminal sagesse, which is the kind imputed to all males, to himself; he assigns himself a double sex ("I am a complete man, having both sexes of the mind"). He never evades in himself what could manifest woman, declaring that he inherited everything from his mother, unreservedly exhibiting a kind of nervous variability which passes in the eyes of common sense as characteristic of women, unprotestingly receiving the accusations or the compliments which betrayed the woman in him,* even conscious of a kind of feminine morphology which he did nothing to correct, quite the contrary: until the age of fifty, a thin, tense, pale figure (he looked like his wife, he would say), then, in old age, the fleshy face of a matron and a seeress.

THE INFRA-SEX   *The idea alone, critical reflection, all the more discredited in that it generally passes for aristocratic, nicely represents a kind of infra-sex, and everything that participates in the pure idea is swept into the realm of the sterile.*

The idea is known as wisdom, but such wisdom is merely a caricature of real wisdom. This is the result of Jacobin wisdom, purely cerebral and isolated from the People, that incubative milieu par excellence: it produces a series of crimes, i.e., the Terror. The theory of Public Safety, of Raison d'État, is discredited by its intellectual character. Better a warm error than a dry truth, better a glorious error than a base truth (theme of the "triumphant loss in emulation of a victory"). Consider the

---

*Eugène Noël to Michelet: "There is a certain amount of woman in you, as in every great artist."

great family of intellectuals: legists, Jesuits, the abstractors, the learned, the witty, the system makers, Goethe the ironist (caricature of fruitful Laughter), Spinoza and Hegel, fatalists. All these militants of reason have but one sex, that of the idea; which is to say they are corpses (perinde ac cadaver), and this death is the worst of all, for it is a dry death.*

LAUGHTER AND THE GIFT OF TEARS   Instinct, popular wisdom, and intuition are, for their part, the archetypes of any female milieu, which, in contrast to the sterile shock of the idea, possesses the true fecundating power.

Laughter, for instance, as opposed to critical irony, is a germinative power; Robespierre, a dry man, trembles before the comic figures: Fabre, Desmoulins. Rabelais, Luther have fecundated their age by joy; conversely, because of Napoleon–Scapin's lack of savoir-rire, France was dominated by the tyrant. The smile possesses a double nature: sarcastic (in Goethe, for example), it is sterile; dreamy, implying a faith which is not credulous (in the Greeks, in the little girl who cradles her doll), it is fruitful, beneficent.

Another milieu of incubation: tears. Tears are a gift; Saint Louis sought them in vain from God; Michelet himself knew the germinative power of tears: not mental tears, tears of metaphor, but tears of water and salt, tears which come to the eyes, to the mouth, to the face; for tears are the liquid milieu of cordial expansion, which as we know is the true generative power.

SEERS: CHILD AND BARBARIAN   A power which has its beneficent figures, just as the critical idea has its demons: first of

*Michelet greatly contributed to the propagation of a superstition still widespread today: the stupid and harmful distinction between "idea" and "feeling"; our anti-intellectuals are still feathering their nests with it.

all, the child. "In the singularly lucid period which separates the two troubled ages (of the nursing period and puberty), children from eight to thirteen have a singular aptitude to apprehend subtle matters." Uniting common sense and intuition, the child becomes the paragon of all Micheletist heroes, anti-intellectual by definition: for example, there is something of the child in Kosciuszko, as there is in Geoffroy Saint-Hilaire; the hero is always a simple man, i.e., in him the female sex (the heart) prevails over and envelops the male power (the idea). Proof a contrario: *the masters of the Revolution, the oversubtle philosophes, failed to possess the profound simplicity of the child. Hence the Revolution could not crown its work, it could not organize Education.***

Another incubative power: the Barbarian. "The word delights me, I accept it . . . Barbarians. Yes, if it means filled with a new sap, living and rejuvenating . . . We have, we Barbarians, a natural advantage; if the upper classes have culture, we have much more vital warmth . . ." This old anti-intellectual theme (already found in Herder) of the beneficent Barbarian here acquires a purely existential value, that of liquid warmth, of new blood, of blood-as-sap.

WARMTH IS DOWN BELOW   *Warmth, as a matter of fact, is set in opposition to "light." Light is a phenomenon of altitude; and insofar as the critical idea implies culture and brightness, it is discredited both by its aristocratic nature and by its icy (sterile) nature. Warmth (i.e., the specific virtue of every act of incubation) is, on the contrary, a phenomenon of depth; it is the sign of the mass, of the innumerable, of the people, of the barbarian. "Our continual invasion, made by us barbarians, is in-*

---

*Contrary to the classical metaphor (Pascal, d'Alembert), Michelet's humanity is not a man who ages; it is a man who grows younger, who has his childhood before him like a paradise.

dispensable to warm those who rise up into a colder, perhaps more luminous atmosphere, by our fecund warmth."

French society, for instance, is constituted by zones of different temperatures, from the incubative milieu par excellence, the people, that warm and enveloping matrix, to the thin and icy air of the upper classes. Once again, the order is reversed: the infra-sex is up above, alone, cold, sterile; the ultra-sex is down below, it is the one which warms, hatches, radiates light. Consider the sequence of the ages of life, Renaissance, eighteenth century, at the heart of a petrified Church: Satan, i.e., Nature, heats the structure of ice: the Church melts from below, it is gradually drawn upward by the warm breath of the Revolution. Consider the People: located at the very bottom of the social ladder, it is the People which is integral warmth, the incubative layer where everything is born.

THE ULTRA-SEX   For the ultra-sex is, in the last analysis, the People. It is the People which possesses, in the ideal state, that combination of wisdom and instinct, that union of the two sexes of the mind, which forms the womb of Good. It is only logical, consequently, to attribute to the People a kind of infallibility. What the People believes is true, what the People does is good. As we have already seen, the national Legend, i.e., the thought of the People, is the true basis of historical credibility. The Historian, by nature of cerebral function—i.e., of male, hence barren sex—finds no truth; it is not he who writes History, it is the People that dictates that History to him; he can claim only to tell the People what the People has done, what the People has conceived, without always understanding the People (by which is meant: intellectually). Hence, the best historian is the one who has emerged from the People, the one who is closest to the People (as Michelet strove so hard to be). In the same way, the institutions of France are not the fruit of its rulers: it

is the power of the People which conceives the Laws, the legis-
lator merely transcribes juridically what the People has decided,
he is merely the clerk of the People (we recall that the scribe is
by nature barren, since he has only the sex of the idea).

HERR OMNES *What, then, is the People for Michelet? It is
Herr Omnes (a phrase of Luther's, quoted by Michelet). Mr.
Everyone. No one to be left out? Yes, all the infra-sexes, the
priests, the legists, the intellectuals. But not the bourgeoisie. No
sociological rigor in Michelet's definition: the People is not a
collection of determined classes,* it is an element defined by its
double sex, its power of incubation, i.e., ultimately, its potential
of warmth. Consider the book* Le peuple: it excludes no one,
strictly speaking; even the rich, in a sense, are part of the People;
simply, here, the warmth is minimal, it is almost the sterile cold
of the upper atmospheres.*
    Since the People is an element and not a social group, there
is no necessity to describe the ethics of each class. Throughout
Micheletist History, there is only one mode of life, which is that
of Michelet himself: all humanity lives in a petit-bourgeois setting; nothing in common with the Balzacian novel, in which
society appears differentiated to extremes, according to the modes
of possession of the classes, where it is Money which determines
to the last degree the various ways of speaking, eating, living,
and loving.*
    It appears that at the beginning, in the para-Christian Ages
of his History (at the moment when he was writing his Middle
Ages), Michelet initially had a conception of the People that was
more ethical than Gnostic: the People here is what is weak,
what suffers, and cannot express itself. Here all the Micheletist
heroes are the vanquished: Godfroy de Bouillon (who dies a*

*Marx: "In 1871 . . . the proletariat and the peasantry constituted the people."
—*The Civil War in France*

virgin and a poor man at the Holy Sepulcher), Thomas Becket, Saint Louis, the peasant Jacques, Jeanne d'Arc. This is because at this time Michelet's morality is entirely subject to the Christian dialectic of reversal: the first will be last, weakness is only the exact seed of a future strength.

YES AND NO   Based on the alliance of the two sexes, the People gradually becomes in Michelet a superior means of knowledge. Quite like Woman, and in virtually the same direction, the People is above History, it opens Nature and grants access to the supernatural goal of a paradisal, reconciled humanity. The conjunction of adverse sexes into a third and complete ultra-sex represents the abolition of all contraries, the magical restoration of a seamless world which is no longer torn between contradictory postulations. The order of contraries is Scholastic, i.e., it belongs to the infra-sex (it will be recalled that reflexive philosophy is in itself sterile). Contrary to this, the beneficent figures of the ultra-sex, the child, the Greek, the peasant, Germany (minus Goethe), the People, set no frontier between yes and no. Michelet, moreover, has given the same image of this higher ambiguity: that of the little girl cradling her doll, smiling at her doll yet knowing all the while that her doll is a wooden figure.

THE PEOPLE IS THE PHILOSOPHERS' STONE   This resolution of contraries is in fact the program of all Gnostics. The People, for Michelet, is the key substance, the life substance which permits overcoming the contradictions which at the time passed for human nature: for example, being both poet and philosopher, active and contemplative, religious and reasoning, sage and child, and, to sum it all up, the final Gnostic ambition, young and old at once.

This Faustian problem (despite our anti-Goethe) here receives a solution entirely in conformity with hermeticism. The notion of a mysterious wisdom, transmitted by initiation and outside of the official philosophies, was a very old one (Plato, Proclus, the sixteenth century, Berkeley, the illuminists of the late eighteenth century). Of this tradition, Michelet retains even the quest for a unique philter, half substance, half warmth, whose ingestion grants the initiate knowledge of a supernatural order, since it is a gaze which abolishes contraries. The philter is the People. Ultimately, the People is for Michelet the philosophers' stone of the hermeticists (moreover, it had a woman's name: opus Virginis Mariae), old Berkeley's tar water, Schelling's oxygen; it is life reduced to its principle, the world unified in one incorruptible kind. Hence, to plunge into the People, to absorb the People, is to ingest the magical substance which keeps one from dying.

THE IMPOSSIBLE LANGUAGE   *Yet, just as all Magicians since Moses have seen the Promised Land without being able to cross into it, so Michelet has seen the People and yet remained at the People's frontier. No matter how often he repeated, in each of his prefaces, that he was born of the People, that the People was his Father, there was always an obstacle to this magical incorporation. And what was that? Speech. "I was born of the people, I have the people in my heart. . . . But the people's language, its language was inaccessible to me. I have not been able to make the people speak . . ."*

Hence Michelet suffers a final failure, and his whole cosmology of redemption involves a distress. What mocking defect appears in this triumphant universe of the seamless and the warm? Nothing but a question of language: to speak like the people. Thus, it is Michelet's entire speech—i.e., his entire work—which bears him, lacerated, far from his paradise: he is perhaps the first author of modernity able to utter only an impossible language.

Well before Law's *System,* Paris becomes one great coffee-house. Three hundred cafés are opened for conversation. There are even cafés in the other big cities—in Bordeaux, Nantes, Lyons, Marseilles, etc.

Notice that every apothecary also sells coffee, and serves it at his counter. Notice that the convents themselves hasten to take part in this lucrative commerce: in the parlor, the extern sister, with her young lay sisters, at the risk of frivolous comment, offers coffee to the visitors.

Never did France talk more, or better. There was less rhetoric than in '89. Wit sprang forth, spontaneous, where it might and as it could.

There is no doubt that the honor of this sparkling explosion belongs in part to the happy revolution of the times, to the great phenomenon which created new habits, even modified temperaments: *the advent of coffee.*

The effect was incalculable, not being weakened, neutralized, as it is today, by the stupefaction of tobacco. Men took a good deal of snuff, men smoked very little.

The *cabaret* is dethroned—the ignoble cabaret where, under Louis XIV, the youth of the day rolled on the floor between the casks and the whores. Fewer drunken songs in the night. Fewer great lords in the gutter. The elegant shop of *causeries,* more salon than shop, changes and ennobles manners: the café's regime is that of temperance.

Coffee, the sober liquor, powerfully cerebral, which, unlike alcohol, increases clarity and lucidity—coffee which suppresses the vague and heavy poetry of the imagination's mists, which strikes a spark from what is actually and accurately seen, the flash of truth itself—the anti-erotic coffee, imposing the alibi of sex by the stimulation of the mind.

In England, coffeehouses open from Charles II (1669) to the ministry of the Cabal, but never assume this character. Alcohol or heavy wines and beers are preferred to coffee.

In France, cafés are opened a little later (1671), without much effect. The Revolution is needed, freedom of speech at the very least.

The three ages of coffee are those of modern thought; they mark the solemn moments of the brilliant *age of wit.*

Arab coffee prepares the way, even before 1700. Those fine ladies you see in the fashions of Bonnard, sipping out of their tiny cups, are imbibing the aroma of the subtlest Arab coffee. And what are they talking about? About Chardin's *Seraglio,* about *coiffures à la sultane,* about *The Thousand and One Nights* (1704). They are comparing the tedium of Versailles to these paradises of the Orient.

Soon (1710) the reign of Indian coffee begins, abundant, popular, relatively cheap. Île-Bourbon, our Indian island, where coffee is planted, experiences an unheard-of good fortune.

This coffee from volcanic soil constitutes the explosion of the Regency and of the new spirit, the sudden hilarity, the mockery of the Old World, the sallies which riddle it, that torrent of sparks of which Voltaire's light verse and Montesquieu's *Persian Letters* give us only a vague notion. Even the most brilliant books could not catch hold of that winged conversation which floats overhead, back and forth, ineffable. It is this Genius of ethereal nature which, in *The Thousand and One Nights,* the enchanter seeks to put into the bottle. But what flask will serve his turn?

The lavas of Île-Bourbon, like the Arabic sands, were insufficient for production. The Regent realized as much, and had coffee shipped to the fertile soil of our Antilles. Two bushes from the King's Garden, carried by the Chevalier de Clieux, with the care, the religious love of a man who felt he was bearing a revolution, arrived in Martinique and succeeded so well that this island was soon yielding ten thousand pounds a year. This powerful coffee, that of Santo Domingo, full-bodied and nourishing, as well as stimulating, fed the adult years of the century, the powerful period of the Encyclopedia. It was drunk by Buffon, by Diderot, by Rousseau, added its warmth to souls already warm, its light to the piercing vision of the prophets assembled in the "cave of Procopius," who saw at the bottoms of their cups of that black brew the future rays of '89.

1863. *Histoire de France,* XV, 8

MELANCHOLY OF MALE LOVE: THE ALOE

"Have you seen the Aloe, that sweet and wild African plant, pointed, bitter, lacerating, which has enormous darts for leaves? It loves and dies every ten years. One morning, the amorous spire, stored so long in the fierce creature, leaps forth with the noise of a gunshot, flinging itself toward the heavens. And this spire is a whole tree which is no less than thirty feet tall, bristling with mournful flowers . . ."

1862. *La sorcière,* I, 7

"So," the wise will say, "abandoning the *terra firma* of the idea, you take your stand upon the shifting paths of sentiment . . ."

To which I should answer: Few, very few ideas are new. Almost all those which burst forth in this century and seek to influence it have appeared many times, but always to no avail. The advent of an idea is not so much the first appearance of its formulation as its definitive incubation, when, received in the powerful warmth of love, it blossoms forth, fecundated by the heart's force.

Then, then, it is no longer a word, it is a living thing; as such, it is loved, embraced, like a dear newborn babe which humanity takes in its arms.

1854. *Les femmes de la Révolution,* Conclusion

ONLY ONE MORE LITTLE CRIME

The Jacobins carried pride to the second power; they worshipped their wisdom. They made frequent appeals to the violence of the people, to the force of their arms. They bought the people, drove the people, but did not consult the people. They made no effort to discover the nature of the popular instincts which were being expressed among the masses against their barbarous system. All that their men were voting in the clubs of '93, in every department, was voted on a watchword from the Holy of Holies in the rue Saint-Honoré. By imperceptible minorities they boldly settled national questions, showed the cruelest disdain for the majority, and believed so fiercely in their own infallibility that, without remorse, they sacrificed to it a world of living men.

And this is more or less what they said: "We are the wise ones, the strong ones; the rest are fools, children, old women. Our doctrine is the true one, even if our number is minimal. Let us save this cattle in spite of itself. What is the difference, if a few more or a few less are killed? Are such creatures sufficiently alive to complain of their deaths? The earth itself will gain by it."

"Only one day of crime . . ." That is what good Louis XI used to say: "Only one more little crime, my good Virgin, only the death of my brother, and the kingdom is saved."

"Only one day of crime, tomorrow the people will be saved; we put Morality and God on the order of the day." In other words: "When we have made this people wretched, giving its name to what is done by a tiny minority, when we have destroyed in that people, by the shameful habits of fear, all moral energy; then, by means of a little proclamation, of a stamped piece of paper, everything will be reborn, everything will rise again; the withered soul of this people will flower again in the sight of Heaven and Earth."

1847. *Histoire de la Révolution,* II, preliminary note

THE STERILE SMILE: GOETHE

[*The Invasion of France: August 1792*]

. . . Here, traveling with the army of the King of Prussia, is the great Mephistopheles of Germany, the doctor of irony, in order to kill by ridicule those whom the sword has left alive. Not for anything in the world would Goethe have missed such an occasion to observe the disappointments of enthusiasm and the fiascos of faith.

1850. *Histoire de la Révolution,* IV, 3

. . . In this army of kings and princes, there was among others a sovereign prince, the Duke of Weimar, and with him his friend, the prince of German thought, as we have said, the famous Goethe. He had come to see the war, and on his way, on the floor of some wagon, he was writing the first fragments of the *Faust* which he published upon his return. This assiduous courtier of public opinion, who expressed it so faithfully, never outstripping it, thereupon described in his fashion the decomposition, the doubt, the discouragement of Germany. He poetized for it, in a sublime work, its moral vacancy, its vigorous agitation of mind. Germany would emerge from it in glory, by such men of faith as Schiller, Fichte, above all by Beethoven. But the time had not yet come.

Ibid., 8

IRONIC GERMANY

. . . My point of view was fraternal toward Germany. Oh, how I loved that Germany; the great and naïve one, the Germany of the Nibelungen and of Luther, of Beethoven and of the good Froebel of the kindergartens. But I loved much less the ironic Germany of Goethe, the sophisticated Germany of Hegel, who has produced its present fatalism. I hoped better of Germany, and I am amazed to see her dead in the midst of her victory, in the iron sepulcher where a Slavic state, Prussia, has inhumed her.

1872. *Origine des Bonaparte,* Preface

FLUIDITY OF THE SMILE

The world's greatest artists, the geniuses who regard nature so tenderly, will here allow me a very humble comparison. Have you ever noticed the touching seriousness of a little girl, innocent yet stirred by her future maternity, who cradles the work of her own hands, animates it with her kiss, and says to it from her heart: *My little girl* . . . If you treat her dolly roughly, she will frown and cry. And yet this does not keep her from knowing the real nature of this being that she animates, makes speak and reason, that she vivifies with her own soul.

A little image and a great thing. Here, precisely, is art in its conception. Here is its essential condition of fecundity. It is love, but it is a smile. It is this loving smile which creates.

If the smile is transcended, if irony begins, harsh criticism and logic itself, then life takes cold, withdraws, contracts, and nothing whatever is produced. The weak, the sterile, all who, trying to create, mingle with their pathetic offspring an *although* and an *unless,* those solemn fools are unaware that no life will rise from that cold milieu; from their icy nothingness will emerge . . . nothingness.

Histoire de France, I, 1869 preface

THE GIFT OF TEARS

I had a splendid malady which darkened my youth, but one quite suitable to the historian. I loved death. I had lived nine years at the gates of Père-Lachaise, then my only promenade. Later I lived near La Bièvre, in the midst of great convent gardens, more sepulchers. I led a life which the world might have called buried, having no society but that of the past, and for friends only the entombed. Re-creating their legend, I wakened in them a thousand vanished things. Certain nursemaids' songs, of which I possessed the secret, were sure of their effect: by such accents, they believed that I was one of theirs. The gift which Saint Louis begged for and never obtained was mine: "the gift of tears."

Histoire de France, I, 1869 preface

Père-Lachaise Cemetery at the time when Michelet
used to take romantic walks there

"The saynted kynge wondrously besought the grace of tears,
and complayned unto his confessor whereby the tears came
to him not, and he sayd unto him meekly, humbly and privily in the litany of words: Sweet Lord God, we pray thee
that thou deign give us the fountayn of tears, the saynted
kynge devoutly prayed: O lord God, I dare not beg for
fountayns of tears suffice it unto me a few drops of tears
that I may moisten the dryness of my heart . . . And many
a time he acknowledged unto his confessor privily that many
a time he gave to our lord tears in prayer: which, when he
did feel them running gently down his countenance and even
entering into his mouth, they seemed to him so savory and
sweet withal, not only to the heart, but to the mouth even."

Le confesseur, quoted by Michelet—1833
Histoire de France, II, 8

. . . All the earth still seemed dressed in a white shroud, captive of a heavy ice, of pitiless crystals, uniform, sharp, and cruel. Especially since 1200, the world was sealed up like a transparent sepulcher in which one sees with terror all things motionless and hardened.

It has been said that "the Gothic church is a crystallization." And this is true. Toward 1300, the architecture, sacrificing its aspect of living caprice, of variety, endlessly repeating itself, rivals with the monotonous prisms of the Spitzberg. True and dreadful image of the hard city of crystal, in which a terrible dogma sought to bury all of life.

But, whatever the supports, buttresses, and reinforcements on whose strength the monument relied, one thing made it tremble. Not noisy blows from without; but something gentle which is in the foundations, which works within this crystal, bringing about a gradual and imperceptible thaw. What is it? The humble stream of warm tears which a world has shed, a sea of tears. Which sea? A breath to come, the powerful, invincible resurrection of the life of nature. The fantastic edifice, of which more than one wall was already crumbling, whispered to itself, but not without terror: "It is the breath of Satan."

Like a glacier of the Hecla on a volcano which has no need to erupt, a warm, slow, kindly hearth which caresses it from beneath calls it to itself, and murmurs to it gently: "Descend."

1862. *La sorcière,* I, 7

WARMTH IS DOWN BELOW

In nations as in geology, warmth is down below. Descend, you will find that it increases; in the lower levels, it is burning hot.

The poor love France, as though having some obligation, having certain duties toward her. The rich love her as though she belonged to them, were obliged to them. The patriotism of the poor is the sentiment of duty; that of the rich, a demand, the claim of a right.

The peasant, as we have said, has married France in a legitimate wedding; she is his wife forever; he is one with her. For the worker, she is his lovely mistress; he has nothing, but he has France, her noble past, her glory. Free of local ideas, he adores the great unity of France. He must be very wretched, enslaved by hunger and hard labor, when this sentiment fails him; never is it extinguished altogether.

The wretched bondage of interests augments still further, if we ascend to the artisans, to the merchants. They inveterately feel in jeopardy, working as though on a tightrope. . . . To avoid what looms as a partial bankruptcy, they risk making it a general one . . . they have created and undone July. . . .

. . . How cold it is, if I ascend still further—it is as though I were in the Alps. I attain the region of the snows. Moral vegetation gradually vanishes, the flower of national consciousness fades. It is a world caught in the sudden chill of egoism and panic. . . . If I mount one degree higher, even fear has ceased, and it is the pure selfishness of the calculator without fatherland that I discover. . . . No more men, only figures. . . . A true glacier abandoned by nature. . . . May I be permitted to come down now, the cold is too great up here for me, I can no longer breathe.

1846. *Le peuple,* I, 8

If my heart were to be opened after I die, there would be read the idea which has pursued me: "How do books come to be of the people?"

Who will write them? A great problem. Three things are required which are very rarely found together. *Genius and charm* (do not imagine that the people can be made to swallow anything insipid, anything weak). A very sure *tact*. And finally (what a contradiction!) there must be a divine *innocence*, the childlike sublimity which one occasionally glimpses in certain young beings, but only for a brief moment, like a flash of heaven.

O problem! to be old and young, both at once, to be a wise man, to be a child!

I have pondered these thoughts all my life. They have been with me always, to my shame and despair. In them I have felt our wretchedness, the impotence of men of letters, of subtle-minded men. I have despised myself.

I was born of the people, I have the people in my heart. The monuments of its olden days have been my delight. In '46 I could posit the people's rights as never before; in '64 the people's long religious tradition. But the people's language, its language was inaccessible to me. I have not been able to make the people speak.

1869. *Nos fils,* V, 2

Michelet around 1865

READING MICHELET

In Michelet's work, there is a critical reality independent of the idea, of the influence, and of the image: it is the theme. How are we to recognize one of Michelet's themes?

REPETITION   *First of all, the theme is* iterative, *i.e., it is repeated throughout the work. Take the opposition of Guelf and Ghibelline (i.e., of Germanity and Latinity, of the vassal and the legist), you will find it ten times in Michelet's work, as often at the beginning as at the end.*

This has two consequences. First of all, we must read Michelet as a polyphony, not only with our eyes but also with our ears, our memory; we must recall, when we encounter the Guelf–Ghibelline pair, that it does not constitute a historical view, but, by its very repetition, the expression of an existential choice. If Michelet institutes this pair at very different moments of his thought, the way a musical theme is lodged in every part of a symphony, it is because he has made it his whole responsibility—that of the body, no longer only that of the mind—to set the cerebral contraction of the legist in opposition to the cordial expansion of the German.

Thus, we must realize that the theme resists History. History—that of his time—could inflect Michelet's ideology, mak-

ing him here the servant of the throne and there a militant anticlerical.* But it could not change his myths. Between 1830 and 1860, Michelet may have changed his opinion about Christianity: meanwhile, there had been the affair of the Jesuits, the spiritual rape of Madame Dumesnil by her confessor, a thousand political or individual circumstances. But confronting these variations on a crucial point of his thought, we must set the fixity of an apparently minor theme, like that of the doll the child believes and does not believe in: you will find it in 1837, in 1849, and in 1858.

The theme's iterative character, moreover, is effective only because there is in Michelet a verbal fixity of themes: they always indicate their presence by the same word or the same image: here the doll, the Dutch canalboat, the sword and the principle, there an adjective (the Dry, the Suspect, the Bizarre, etc.) which possesses the same algebraic power as a veritable epithet of nature. The "dry" Louis XV is not only a moral estimation, it is the index of a certain nausea, the kind which is attached to a discontinuous substance.

SUBSTANCE *The theme is in effect* substantial, *it brings into play an attitude of Michelet's with regard to certain qualities of matter: the historical object can always be reduced to the disgust, the attraction, or the bewilderment it produces. The Barbarian, a common romantic entity, is constituted in Michelet by a certain state of substance, it is the historic figure of the fluid and of the genetic, it is an undivided and enveloping element. In contrast, the Jesuit is always recalled as an algebraic representation of the machine, i.e., of the Dry, of an absence of links of substance.*

The theme's substantial character involves two consequences:

*Proudhon (1858): "What a prodigious distance this man has come! A zealous Catholic under the Restoration, today a revolutionary like you and me."

first of all, the theme keeps History afloat. For example, politically, Michelet had no original views, he had only the average ideas of the petite-bourgeoisie around 1840. But transformed into themes, these common ideas become specific experiences: Anglophobia is sustained by a nausea of the sanguinary plethora, of motionless blood; Germanophilia, on the contrary, by the delicious taste of infinite fluence, of milk-blood; the mechanical is discredited by the horror attached to the Dry and to the Sterile; and the People is redemption to the degree that it is ultra-sex, alliance of the male-idea and the female-sentiment. Thus, the Micheletist theme has two roots: a historical root and an existential root. This is why historical criticism should not concern itself with Michelet without first having established his thematics.

Thus, the theme sustains a whole system of values; no theme is neutral, and all the substance of the world is divided up into beneficent and maleficent states. Contrary to current opinion, Michelet's morality is not at all rhetorical; it is a morality of the body; History is judged at the tribunal of the flesh: Good is determined by virtue of its seamless, fluid, rhythmic nature, and Evil as a consequence of its dryness and its discontinuity.

REDUCTION *Lastly, the theme is reducible. The Barbarian, the Child, Tears are themes reducible to the choice of a round, moist warmth. The Jesuit, the Machine, Tedium, the Novel are multiplications of a common element: dry death. Hence, Michelet's history is covered by a network of themes, which connect by relations of dependency and reduction. A veritable algebra is constituted, for each theme can be presented in an elliptical form. A reading of Michelet is total only if we distinguish the themes, and if we can set under each of them the memory of its substantial signification and of the other themes to which it is linked.*

Man-of-the-Wind: François I, *by Titian*

"The light creature is so naturally mendacious that in him the lie is less an action than the instinctive efflorescence of a character altogether false. He is a living fib, a comedy, a farce, a legend, a fable. The Spanish *hablero* does not even express this—I prefer the Latin *vanus*. Yes, he is *vanus* and *vanitas.*" —*Histoire de France,* VIII

Whale-Man: Ruyter, *by Jordaens*

"He is Gargantua in girth, half whale and half man. His big black eyes
protruding from his red face, so proudly colored up, fling forth a rushing
stream of life, a fearful good humor, and the contagion of victory."

—*Histoire de France,* IX, 7

Finding in Michelet the notion of "phantasmagoria," we must recall that the phantasmagoria is linked to two thematic "paths": that of the intermittent, of the indeterminate, the suspect, the equivocal, the unhealthy, the murky, the bizarre, i.e., of an unstable state of substance, and that of Gaming, of the arbitrary, of pretense, of Italian farce, i.e., of Grace and of the World-as-Woman. It is only at the end of these two implicit systems of references that we can understand why the phantasmagoria totally discredits Napoleon.

Another example of the thematic network: Callisthenes, Aristotle's nephew, is crucified by order of Alexander. We have not read this sentence if we fail to remember that Aristotle, established as the philosopher of energy, here represents the theme of action, and Alexander that of Gaming, of Grace, and of monarchic turgidity; which comes down to setting in opposition, once again, male Justice and female Grace.

Hence, it is not excessive to speak of a veritable hermeneutics of the Micheletist text. We cannot read Michelet in a linear fashion, we must restore to the text its strata and its network of themes: Michelet's discourse is a kind of cryptogram, we must make it into a grid, and this grid is the very structure of the work. It follows that no reading of Michelet is possible if it is not total: we must resolutely locate ourselves within the closure.

Michelet's second wife was mistaken: she understood nothing of her husband's work, because she read only its surface rhetoric, and because she collected only the (weak) ideas, without seeing the (constant) themes. This is revealed in the way she falsified Michelet's manuscripts, stupidly falsifying the themes, i.e., Michelet himself. Here is one example, a text of Michelet's retouched by his wife: it will be noticed that the only Micheletist element of the text, the moist warmth of the Dutch vessel, has been foolishly eliminated. Contrasting with this blindness, we must consider Proust's perspicacity in parodying Michelet, and his capacity to rediscover not only the verbal tics but also the secret themes.

Manuscript	*Falsified, Published Text*
Beauty of the barbarous costume, gold plates harmonizing with the blond hair; gentleness and excellence of the women. Frequently a bit mannish, broad-shouldered, strong-backed. One must see them on the boats, hanging out wash, caring for the children, even holding the tiller. Now I understand the huge, curved Dutch boat, so thoroughly decked over. It is Noah's ark which must contain a whole family, men, women, children, animals. The boat is a house, washed continually, as if it were not wet enough. The Dutchman living on the water, in perpetual migration, makes it a land of his own. It matters little to him if he gets there quickly or not, provided he does not endanger his little world . . . We must not ridicule him; the perpetual washings, the planting of trees one might think less appropriate to such a climate, are quite intentional. Both purify, in different ways. It is less the humidity which spoils things than the decomposition to which it gives rise. The canals are corrosive	Frisia still retains the beauty of the barbarous costume; on the women's foreheads gleam the gold plates harmonizing so well with the gentle warmth of their blond hair. Here one can grasp the difference between past and present. Once, for the sailors, struggle took the place of any kind of idea. After the struggle against the foreigner and against nature was over, materialism prevailed among this people and stupefied it. The sailors, once they took to terra firma, seem to have lost all sense of activity. They spend their days in the taverns, drinking and playing cards. We are better off venturing into one of these Dutch barges, waiting for their moment of departure. You are struck with admiration. While the man is resting, the sailor's wife takes all the work on herself. At first glance you will find her too broad-shouldered, too mannish in her ways. But watch her in action and in her element, on her boat, washing the deck, hanging up the wash, caring for the children, the animals, even holding the tiller; then

enough, but what can be done about it? —They smoke, drink, etc. Now that the struggle against Spain is over, and the struggle against nature, their natural materialism has lulled them to sleep. Descartes and Spinoza, two foreigners, express well enough both the struggle and the absorption.
—Travel notes of 1837. Quoted in J.-M. Carré, *Michelet et son temps*

you will understand that strength in her arms and in her shoulders, you will understand her, and you will admire her.
—*Sur les chemins de l'Europe.* Posthumous

L'Affaire Lemoine

The diamond can be extracted at strange depths (1,300 meters). In order to delve for the dazzling stone, which alone can match the fire in a woman's eyes (in Afghanistan the diamond is called "eye of flame"), unremittingly one must descend into the dark realm. How many times Orpheus will lose his way before bringing Eurydice up to the light! Yet there must be no discouragement. If the heart weakens, the stone is there, which with its distinct, irregular flame seems to say: "Courage, one more shovelful, and I am yours!" Moreover, the recompense for hesitation is death. Salvation lies in speed alone. An affecting dilemma. In order to resolve it, countless lives were lost in the Middle Ages. Yet it was again proposed all the more harshly at the beginning of the twentieth century (December 1907–January 1908). Someday I shall describe that magnificent Affaire Lemoine, whose significance no contemporary has so much as suspected; I shall show that tiny man, with his weak hands, his eyes scorched by the terrible quest, a Jew most likely (M. Drumont has asserted as much with a certain show of truth: even today the Lemoustiers—a contraction of Monastère—are not rare in the Dauphiné, a chosen site of Israel during the Middle Ages), for three months secretly controlling European politics, compelling proud England to agree to a disastrous commercial treaty, in order to save her threatened mines, her collapsing corporations. Were we to yield up this man to her, no doubt she would pay for his weight without one moment's hesitation—his weight in diamonds! Temporary freedom, the greatest conquest of modern times (Sayous, Batbie), thrice was rejected. Germany, deducing powerfully over her steins, seeing daily the De Beers stocks falling, mustered her courage (review of the Haren case, Polish laws, refusal to answer the Reichstag). Touching immolation of the Jew down through the ages! "Stubbornly you calumny me, accuse me of treason against all appearances, on earth, at sea [Affaire Dreyfus, Affaire Ullmo]; well then! I give you my gold [see the enormous development of Jewish banks at the end of the nineteenth century], and more than gold, what at gold's weight you cannot always buy: the diamond." A serious lesson; how sadly I brooded upon it, and how often during the winter of 1908 when nature herself, renouncing all violence, turned perfidious. Never has one seen fewer cold spells, but a mist which at high noon the sun failed to penetrate. Moreover, a very balmy temperature—all the more murderous. Many dead—more than during the ten preceding years—and in January violets under the snow. My mind very disturbed by this Affaire Lemoine, which quite justly struck me at once as an episode of the great struggle of wealth against science, every day I went to the Louvre, where instinctively the people, more often than in front of Da Vinci's *Gioconda,* halted before the diamonds of the Crown. More than once I had difficulty approaching them. Need I say, this study lured me—I did not seek it out. The secret of this? I did not feel life within it. Always this was my strength, my weakness as well, this need for life. At the culminating point of the reign of Louis XIV, when absolutism seems to have slain all freedom in France, during two long years—more than a century—(1680–1789), strange headaches made me believe each day that I would be compelled to interrupt my history. Indeed, I recovered my powers only at the Tennis Court Oath (June 20, 1789). Similarly, I was feeling troubled before this strange kingdom of crystallization which is the world of stone. Here no more of that flexibility of the flower which in the most arduous periods of my botanical research, quite timidly—so much the better—never ceased to sustain my courage: "Have confidence, fear nothing, you are still alive, still in life, in history."

—Marcel Proust, *Pastiches et Mélanges,* 1919

REVIEW OF THE CHIEF THEMES CITED

I Maleficent Themes

Themes of the Dry

The Machine
The Jesuit
The Scribe
The Jacobin
The Scholastics
Public Safety
Irony (Goethe)
Fatalism (Hobbes, Molinos, Spinoza, Hegel)
Minerality
Dried, hardened, virginal blood
The Electric

Themes of the Empty and the Turgid

Middle Ages
The Imitation
Tedium
The Novel
Narcotics
Alexander
Plethoric, engorged blood

Themes of the Indeterminate

The *Honnête-Homme*
Condé, Chantilly, Sade
Gambling
Phantasmagoria
Italian comedy
White blood, sealed blood

II Beneficent Themes

Themes of the Fecund

(Penetration:)
Action
Education
The Stoics
Energy (18th cent.)
Laughter
Satan, the Witch
The Hero

Themes of the Warm

(Incubation:)
Believing and not believing (the doll)
Tears
The Dutch canalboat
The Barbarian
The Child
Germany
The People
Flowing, rhythmic blood

III Paired Themes

Union and Unity
Prose and Poetry
Guelfs and Ghibellines
Grace and Justice
Heart and Reason

WHAT WAS SAID ABOUT MICHELET BY . . .

Victor Hugo to Michelet

Hauteville-House, July 14 (1860)

I have just received your book,* and I have read it through, without drawing a breath. Men like you are essential; since the centuries are so many sphinxes, we must have our Oedipuses to face them down. You come to these dark riddles, and you speak the dread word. This fraudulent century of ours, this fraudulent reign had to be unmasked, the wig that concealed the death's-head had to be snatched off, the crime revealed beneath the purple. This you have done. I thank you for it. Yes, I thank you for this book as for a personal favor. This Louis XIV weighs upon me; in a poem as yet unpublished,† I have spoken of him as you have. I cherish this agreement between our two souls.

All your books are acts. As a historian, as a philosopher, as a poet, you win battles. Progress and Thought will count you among their heroes. And what a painter you are! You bring that reign to life before you decapitate it. I must end this letter, but it is to return to your book; I am not leaving you.

Dear great thinker, I embrace you.

Victor Hugo
—Quoted in J.-M. Carré, *Michelet et son temps*

*Histoire de France, XIII.
†Quatre vents de l'esprit, Livre Épique: La Révolution

Tonight, December 20, 1870, M.P., dining in my house, told me: "Do you know why Michelet has left Paris? —No. —Because you are going there. —Nonsense! —He wants to be alone in Paris. With you there, one of you is *de trop*. —But why? —He is jealous. —Oh, jealous: is he afraid I will sleep with his wife? —No, he's afraid you'll sleep with his glory."

—Pierres, Geneva

SAINTE-BEUVE (I)

I shall undertake here neither criticism nor eulogy of this way of writing history, as remote as possible, I confess, from my own tastes, my own habits. Let it be sufficient for me to say that M. Michelet has made it his own by dint of will and of talent, that he has wrought it to a point where it is unique, that he has now become a past master in his style; and since advice would be especially futile, I accept the man of knowledge, of imagination, and of heart for what he is; I take him in the brilliant and venturesome products which he has given us; I mourn what shocks me here, I render justice and homage to so many wonderful passages, from which I have benefited. In a word, M. Michelet is an established power; *I have resisted it long enough, despite my old friendship for the man, I capitulate:* I acknowledge it at last, this power, and only ask not to dispute it.

—Quoted in J.-M. Carré, Michelet et son temps

SAINTE-BEUVE (II)

I implore Olivier to beware of Michelet. He is a charlatan, disarming people by making up to them and engaging them by *his* praises or by theirs . . . He has already won over *all* the papers here; let us keep the *Revue Suisse* out of his hands. He is a dreary figure really, as I have noticed in all those who are *puffed up. Omnia serviliter pro laude.*

—Quoted in J.-M. Carré, *Michelet et son temps*

THE "ARTISTS": HUYSMANS

. . . For Durtal, history was therefore the solemnest lie of all, the most childish of cheats . . . The truth is that precision is impossible, he reminded himself; how to penetrate the events of the Middle Ages, when no one is in a position even to explain the most recent episodes, the motives of the Revolution, the foundations of the Commune, for example. There is nothing left but to create one's own vision, to imagine to oneself the creatures of another day and age, to incarnate oneself in them, to pull on, if one can, the appearance of their habiliments, in other words to create for oneself, with cunningly sifted details, fallacious ensembles. This is what Michelet has actually done; and although this old bundle of nerves has singularly strayed among the outworks, stopping over trifles, raving gently in anecdotes which he has puffed up and declared to be enormous, once his fits of sentiment and his chauvinism blurred the possibility of his presumptions and downed the health of his conjectures, he was nonetheless the only man in France who had soared above the ages and plunged from on high into the dim chasm of the old narratives.

Hysterical and garrulous, insolent and intimate, his History of France was nonetheless, at certain points, raised up by a wind from the open sea, his characters lived, emerged from that limbo where the ashen anecdotes of his confrères had buried them; it mattered little henceforth that Michelet had been the least accurate of historians, since he was the most personal and the most artistic . . .

—*Là-bas,* 1891

. . . All these so-called contradictions of Michelet, she said, nota-
bly in the history of the Middle Ages, derive from this. From the
fact that sometimes subjugated by modern ideas, by so-called modern
methods, he goes about his work; and then he is in history, in
what we call inscription. But swept away by one of the greatest
geniuses that there has ever been, he suddenly overflows, he creates a work, and then he is in memory, and in aging. Then he is
released. When he follows his times, he is only a historian. When
he follows his genius, he becomes a memorialist and a chronicler.

When he says that history is a resurrection and when he is
made to say as much, he follows his genius and we must understand that from history and from inscription, from historical history, he himself falls back upon memorialist history, upon chroni-
cles, upon memory and aging.

When he says that *history is a resurrection,* and when it is said
so often after him, it means very specifically that we must not pass
along the cemetery, or along the walls of the cemetery, or even
along the *monuments,* but that still situated in the same race, both
fleshly and spiritual, and temporal and eternal, it is a matter of
simply evoking *the ancients.* And of invoking them. The ancients
of the same race. The ancients *in* the same race. Situated, moreover, at a moving point in that race, it is a matter of returning by
an inner gaze to that race itself, of catching up with the backward
members of the race; and one can do this only by an operation of
memory and of aging.

—*Clio,* 1914

THE MARXISTS: MATHIEZ

Michelet, steeped in mysticism, invoked a vague Providence; to all
the evils whose cause he grasped so vaguely, he proposed but one
remedy: education. No doubt he felt a certain sympathy for the

miseries of the people, but to bring them to an end, he could do no more than give himself up to complaints and objurgations which border on the absurd. In an age when Marx was writing the *Communist Manifesto,* he was bleating about the union of classes. Far from having nourished the democratic opposition, he tended to exhaust it, and certainly misled it. Because he lived the first years of his life in his father's print-shop, he prided himself on being one of the people. An unwarrantable claim. He early frequented certain gilded salons, he was the tutor of the princesses of the blood, those of the legitimate monarchy as well as those of the usurping one. In reality, he was one of those fine fruits of that classical education which the sons of the bourgeoisie received in the schools of the period; fruits of striking colors but often hollow within. I am struck by the incoherence and by the frequent banality of his thought. This amateur of philosophy never managed to become a philosopher.

—Quoted in A. Chabaud, *Jules Michelet,* 1929

AND WHAT IS SAID
ABOUT HIM TODAY BY . . .

(1953) JEAN DUVIGNAUD

Michelet is unequaled: no one can be compared to him in the acuity of his dramatic vision, the quasi-Shakespearian grasp of the event as it impinged on the lives of those who created it. This great "stage director" knows how to manage the shadows. He writes for that invisible spectator who is no longer the God of the Hebrews to whom Agrippa d'Aubigné dedicated his *Tragiques,* but History. The "positivists" blamed him for errors in detail, yet they can only bow before the force of his vision. He is truly the Historian in the sense in which history is, for the man who writes it, a way of becoming destiny and not a science. Like Saint-Simon, he can accommodate greatness and still suspect trickery. He casts his characters, without reducing them to what he thinks of them, onto what Piscator would call the *Schicksalsbühne,* the proscenium of fatality. Beside him keeps watch and is transformed that great being he calls France, whose convulsions, incomprehensible to the Great Judge, are nonetheless dedicated to Him alone: the immense, quasi-Dostoevskyan melancholy of a race which torments and punishes itself, intensifies its suffering and its joy beneath the icy gaze of a history which resembles the God of the Bible.

—*Théâtre populaire,* No. 1 (May–June 1953)

Few men continued to trust more naïvely than Michelet in a few simple ideas: in his eyes, the progress of Truth and of Justice and the return to the laws of Nature were guaranteed fulfillment. His work is in this sense a splendid act of faith. But if he had little awareness of the limits of reason, the tendencies which opposed it—this is the paradox which attracts me—sometimes found an accomplice in him. *La sorcière* is doubtless an accidental work—evidently, a few dossiers hitherto unused, gathered up over the years, determined its organization—*La sorcière* makes its author one of those who have spoken most humanly of *evil.*

It seems to me that he was going astray. The paths he was following—at random, guided by "unhealthy" curiosity—nonetheless led in our eyes to our truths. These paths, it is incontestable, are those of *evil.* Not of the common *evil* that we do, abusing strength at the expense of the weak: on the contrary, of that *evil* committed against our own interest, demanded by an imperious desire for freedom. Michelet doubtless saw here a detour taken by the *good.* He attempted as best he could to legitimate it: the witch was a victim and died in the horror of the flames. It was natural to invert the values of the theologians. Wasn't *evil* on the side of the executioner? The witch incarnated a wretched humanity, persecuted by the powerful. These views, no doubt somewhat justified, risked a priori keeping the historian from seeing any further. But his plea conceals a profound venture. What apparently guided Michelet was the vertigo of *evil,* a kind of bewilderment.

. . . He gave to the world he was representing more than a character of rebellion: a higher concern to assure the future, duration. Hence, he limited the freedoms of procedure which constituted the meaning of that world. Let it be said without trying to diminish him (I should like to suggest, on the contrary, a sentiment of power) that Michelet's own life answered to this ambiguity. He was obviously guided by a certain anguish—even led astray by it—while he was writing a book or burning with a dark passion. In a passage of his *Journal* (which I have been unable to read, it is not accessible, but on this point I have obtained from others adequate details) he says that in the course of his labors it would happen that inspiration failed him: he then would go downstairs and out of his house, and enter a public urinal whose odor was suffocating. He breathed deeply, and having thus "approached as close as he could to the object of his horror," he returned to his work. I cannot help recalling the author's countenance, noble, emaciated, the nostrils quivering.

—Preface to *La sorcière*

(1946) LUCIEN FEBVRE
[*In 1846, Michelet publishes* Le peuple]

. . . All those who had made a revolution in 1830 to restore France to her prestige—all those who had taken to the streets in order to defend the rights of an assembly which they did not elect or of a press which they did not read, but above all, to wash away that stain, 1815, which blemished France, and to reject a shame harder to bear for any son of good family than hunger, prison, and embarrassment—all those who did not accept the powerful watchwords of Digestion, Get Rich, or of Prudence, Save Your Skins— all those devoured the burning pages Michelet offered them, with a thrill which a hundred years later we Frenchmen of 1938, of 1940, of 1942, of 1944, we the outraged witnesses of Munich, the stunned witnesses of the disaster, the disgusted witnesses of the usurpation and, if it must be said, even more, the sometimes despairing witnesses of the incomprehension, the excessive incomprehension of the only ones who were offering to help us, we feel as powerfully as our ancestors, those who read *La peuple* when its ink was fresh.

—*Michelet*

CHRONOLOGICAL OUTLINE

The outline that follows does not constitute a general overview of Michelet's life and work; it is intended merely to place him as the author of the *Histoire de la Révolution Française*. Whence its division into three sections: before, during, and after that *History*.

BEFORE

1798   Aug. 21: Birth of Jules Michelet
1810   Sent to the Pension Melot
1812   Enters the Lycée Charlemagne
1817   May 15: Bachelier ès lettres
1818   July 8: Licence ès lettres
1819   Docteur ès lettres upon presentation of the French thesis *Examen des "Vies des Hommes Illustres" de Plutarque* and of the Latin thesis *De percipienda infinitate secundum Lockium*
1821   Oct. 13: Assistant at the Lycée Charlemagne
1822   Assistant in history at the new Collège Sainte-Barbe (later the Collège Rollin)
1824   Marries Mlle Pauline Rousseau
1825   Publishes *Tableau chronologique de l'Histoire Moderne* (1453–1789)
1827   Feb. 3: Appointed professor of philosophy and history at the École Préparatoire, created in 1826 to replace the École Normale suppressed in 1822. Publishes *Précis de l'Histoire Moderne* and a translation of Vico's *Principles of the Philosophy of History*

1831 Publishes *Histoire romaine* in 2 volumes and *Introduction à l'Histoire Universelle*. Appointed section chief at the Archives Nationales

1833 Publishes the first 2 volumes of the *Histoire de France* (from the year 1 to 1270), and *Précis de l'Histoire de France jusqu'à la Révolution*

1834 Jan. 9: Opening lecture at the Sorbonne, where he replaces Guizot

1835 Publishes a translation of Luther's memoirs and an edition of Vico's selected works

1836 Presents a report to the Minister of Public Instruction on the libraries and archives of southwestern France

1837 Publishes *Origines du droit français, cherchées dans les symboles et formules du droit universel,* and Volume III of the *Histoire de France* (1270–1380)

1838 April 23: Chair of History at the Collège de France

1839 Death of his first wife

1840 May 5: First visit to Mme Dumesnil. Publishes Volume IV of the *Histoire de France* (1380–1422). An edition of the *Oeuvres de M. Michelet* begins to appear in Brussels

1841 Publishes, in collaboration with Quinet, *Des Jésuites,* and on December 4 completes Volume VI of the *Histoire de France* (Louis XI and Charles the Bold)

1845 Publishes *Du prêtre, de la femme, de la famille*. An American translation of the first volumes of the *Histoire de France* appears in New York

1846 Death of Michelet's father. He publishes *Le peuple*

DURING

1847 Feb. 10: Publication of the first volume of the *Histoire de la Révolution française* (books I and II). Feb.–March: Lectures on *"Mirabeau et l'esprit de la Révolution"* at the Collège de France. July: Travels in Holland. Aug.: Sojourn in Normandy. Oct. 13: First letter from Athénaïs Mialaret to Michelet. Nov. 15: Volume II on sale (Books III and IV). Dec.: Lectures at the Collège de France on *"La rénovation sociale et la Révolution"*

1848   Jan. 2: Michelet's lectures at the Collège de France are suspended by government order. Feb. 24: The Revolution breaks out. March 6: Resumes his lectures. July 21: Begins writing Volume III of the *Histoire de la Révolution française*. Nov. 8: Athénaïs Mialaret appears at Michelet's residence

1849   Jan. 19: Finishes volume III. Jan. 25: Begins his lectures at the Collège de France on *"L'amour et l'èducation,"* dedicated to Athénaïs Mialaret, who becomes his wife. Feb. 10: Volume III (Books V and VI). March 5: Leaves his Quartier Latin apartment for an apartment in the Quartier des Ternes. March 12: Marries Athénaïs Mialaret. Aug.: Travels in Belgium and the Ardennes. Dec. 27: Begins his lectures at the Collège de France on *"L'éducation populaire et la femme"*

1850   Jan. 22: Volume IV of the *Histoire de la Révolution française* is finished (Books VII and VIII). Feb. 10: It goes on sale. March 10: Begins writing Volume V. July 2: Birth of Michelet's son. Aug. 24: The child dies. Sept.: Sojourn at Fontainebleau. Dec. 26: Resumes his lectures at the Collège de France (same subject as the year before)

1851   Feb.: The administrator of the Collège de France informs the Minister of demonstrations hostile to Louis-Napoléon Bonaparte which occur during Michelet's lectures. March 11: Summoned before a council of his peers. March 13: His lectures are suspended. April 18: Volume V of the *Histoire de la Révolution française* is finished (Books IX and X) and is put on sale almost at once. March 20: Demonstration of students against the suspension of Michelet's lectures. April 8: His salary is suspended. June 17: Meeting with Herzen. July: Journeys to Bordeaux and to Arcachon. Oct. 24: Refuses to accept half salary

1852   March 25: Begins writing Volume VI. April 11: Officially removed from his post at the Collège de France. May 12: Leaves the Quartier des Ternes and settles in Battignolles. June 3: Abstains from taking the oath imposed on officials. June 9: Resigns from his functions at the Archives. June 12: Leaves for Nantes. July 2: Continues writing Volume VI

1853   Feb.–March: Michelet ill. June: Sojourn in Paris. Aug. 1: *L'Histoire de la Révolution française* is finished. Nov.: Sojourn in Italy

1854 Publishes *Les femmes de la Révolution*
1855 Publishes Volumes VII and VIII of the *Histoire de France* (Renaissance and Reformation)
1856 Publication of Volumes IX and X (Wars of Religion, the League, and Henri IV)
1857 Publication of Volume XI (Henri IV and Richelieu)
1858 Publication of Volume XII (Richelieu and the Fronde)
1860 Publication of Volume XIII (Louis XIV and the revocation of the Edict of Nantes)
1861 Publication of *La mer*. Publication of Volume XIV of the *Histoire de France* (Louis XIV and the Duke of Burgundy). Publication of *La sorcière*
1863 Publication of Volume XV of the *Histoire de France* (the Regency)
1864 Publishes under the title *La bible de l'humanité* an essay on the philosophy of the history of religions
1866 Publication of Volume XVI of the *Histoire de France* (Louis XV, 1724–57)
1867 Publication of Volume XVII of the *Histoire de France* (Louis XV and Louis XVI)
1868 Publishes *La montagne*
1871 Protests the annexation of Alsace and Lorraine by Germany in a brochure, *La France devant l'Europe*
1872 Publishes the first volume of the *Histoire du XIXe siècle*
1874 Feb. 9: Death of Michelet at Hyères